EMBRACE YOUR EMOTIONS

A WOMAN'S GUIDE TO
LOWERING STRESS, IMPROVING
RELATIONSHIPS, AND FINDING JOY

EMBRACE YOUR EMOTIONS

SHERESE SHY-HOLMES

Embrace Your Emotions © Copyright 2023 Sherese Shy-Holmes All rights reserved. No part of this publication may be reproduced, distributed, or transmitted in any form or by any means, including photocopying, recording, or other electronic or mechanical methods, without the prior written permission of the publisher, except in the case of brief quotations embodied in critical reviews and certain other noncommercial uses permitted by copyright law.

Although the author and publisher have made every effort to ensure that the information in this book was correct at press time, the author and publisher do not assume and hereby disclaim any liability to any party for any loss, damage, or disruption caused by errors or omissions, whether such errors or omissions result from negligence, accident, or any other cause.

Adherence to all applicable laws and regulations, including international, federal, state, and local governing professional licensing, business practices, advertising, and all other aspects of doing business in the US, Canada, or any other jurisdiction is the sole responsibility of the reader and consumer.

Neither the author nor the publisher assumes any responsibility or liability whatsoever on behalf of the consumer or reader of this material. Any perceived slight of any individual or organization is purely unintentional.

The resources in this book are provided for informational purposes only and should not be used to replace the specialized training and professional judgment of a health care or mental health care professional.

Neither the author nor the publisher can be held responsible for the use of the information provided within this book. Please always consult a trained professional before making any decision regarding treatment of yourself or others.

For more information, email ask@thebizdoula.com ISBN: (print only)

BEFORE YOU START READING, DOWNLOAD YOUR FREE DIGITAL GIFT

Visit the website below to access your free gifts included with your book purchase

To include a meditation to relieve stress.
www.thebizdoula.com/freegifts

To my grandparents, the giants that allowed us to stand on their shoulders.

CONTENTS

INTRODUCTION..10

THINGS I WISHED I'D KNOWN

01. I Got a Big Ego...15
02. What U Workin' With?..26
03. I'm Emotional and I Can't Let Go.........................35
04. Self-Love, Self-Care . . . AF................................43
05. If You're Happy and You Know It........................52

HOW I REALLY LIVED

06. Shame—The TRIGGER of All My Buttons..............67
07. Anger—Detonate in Case of Threat.....................75
08. Unforgiveness—You Can't Change How I Feel......80
09. Grief—How Am I Supposed to Live Now?.............86
10. Settling—I Think I'll Stay Awhile...........................94
11. Stress—I'm Super Woman, and I Don't Need to Rest......102
12. Anti-Self—I Wish I Was (Fill in the Blank).............109
13. Comparison—It's the Pictures for Me...................116
14. Loneliness—But I Love Myself.............................125
15. Anxiety—Let's Get it Poppin'...............................132
ABOUT THE AUTHOR...142

"Until you make the unconscious conscious, it will direct your life and you will call it fate."
—Carl Jung

INTRODUCTION

I used to reject and suppress my emotions, and although I hated crying in front of other people, I was a "crybaby," and to be honest, I still am. Over time I wanted to develop a stoic, strong, resilient persona that told the world "I can take what you got, I'm not scared." But all those years of trying to be the tough girl who managed her emotions, had a stern poker face, and had relentless drive- caught up to me.

It started out small—having a quick temper, taking over projects so I could ensure the best outcome, over-volunteering, and doing all the things. I was left in a cycle of trapped emotions, and the only emotion I thought was acceptable to release was anger. But deep down, I was bitter, resentful, anxious, and completely exhausted from keeping up the stoic front for everyone.

To put it blatantly, my persona of Stoic Sherese was my "representative." A representative is a person chosen to act or speak on the behalf of another. Although the representative may mirror some of the beliefs of who they represent, they never represent one individual; they represent the collective. So I bet you're wondering what was included in my collective. Here's a short list:

Everyone else's feelings and needs are more important than mine.

I have to be super nice so other people will be nice to me.

Being there for other people is more important to me than my mental health, self-esteem, health, or safety.

I have to be good and perfect in order to be accepted and loved.

I gave my representative these commands, and she performed quite well for many years.

I then placed myself in those exact same shoes, well, my representative was, that is. The thing about representatives is that they are very similar to facades, and we all know that eventually, all facades start cracking and need repair. For a long time, that's what I did. I found whatever glue or tape I needed to repair it and held it together by maintaining a positive attitude, using my sheer willpower, or trying to harness my anger for change, but none of it lasted.

Then, in a series of unfortunate events, I systematically had the bottom fall out from underneath me. Before I knew it, I was going through a depressing divorce (which triggered the heart-wrenching pain of community disapproval), a dramatic car crash, and multiple urgent care visits for severe asthma. My life and body were falling apart, and I had to do something fast if I wanted to survive.

The first thing I knew to do was to lean on my faith in God. I was at my lowest point in life, and I literally had no one to turn to—no family and no friends. I felt like completely giving up because nothing seemed to work. In that moment, when I told God that I surrendered, while kneeling on a hardwood floor with the ugliest cry full of snot and tears, I finally felt relief. From that point forward, my spiritual journey changed. I realized my thoughts were out of control, and I'd lost sight of how I truly felt. I got reconnected spiritually, renewed my mind, and began appreciating and integrating my emotions into the decision process. But first and foremost, I know it was God who showed me the path to healing.

I'm aware that everyone doesn't believe in God, so I'm giving you full disclosure here that I do talk about God in the book. But don't let that stop you from reading because I share great information to help you transform how you view your emotions and live a happy and healthier life. I'm sharing what worked for me and what has made me the woman I am today, and I wouldn't have made it this far without God. Each of us has our own unique journey and story, and I honor everyone's story as their own, without stripping it of what's most important to them. I hope that you can do the same: enjoy the journey and take the nuggets that most apply to you.

Every chapter in this book is part of what I learned in my journey. I had to first get acquainted with the functions of the mind and what emotions meant and then apply them. As I did so, the anger I used as my armor began to disintegrate, and I started getting comments from friends and family that my joy was so vibrant that it was like I turned into a completely different person. I gained a new level of confidence in my career and started winning awards and earning bonuses.

Through it all, the most important thing I learned is that emotions, good or bad, are really just signals. Signals given to us to interpret and take appropriate action. The sooner we learn how to interpret them, the less frustrating our responses and decisions will be.

So, here's your call to action: stop playing small and let go of the version of you that you've tried to perfect for others. Lean into you who truly are; reconnect with your deeper self, your emotions, and your body; and PRACTICE, PRACTICE, PRACTICE. I didn't learn the concepts in this book by trying them one time and giving up. You may not get it right every time or you may only do it partly right; in any case, keep working on you. Just don't give up! You will see results when you continue to practice and apply what you're learning.

Take notes, review each chapter, and spend time thinking about how you can apply it to your life. To help you identify how you can apply the material in the chapter, I created a workbook as a companion for the book. Since I learn best through visual aids, I have provided prompts and charts. Please take full advantage of the book by purchasing the workbook.

My hope for you is that this book will be the seed that you needed to plant or the water that you needed to grow. If no one sees your changes, compliments you on your growth, or recognizes your improvement, know that I wrote this book for you and I'm celebrating your fearless growth! Cheers to beautiful beginnings and manifesting your higher self.

Embrace Your Beautiful Emotions!

Your Biggest Fan,

Sherese

P.S. Don't forget to claim your free gift at https://www.thebizdoula.com/freegift

And Stay Connected With Me

Blog: https://www.thebizdoula.com

(Click on "Contact Me" to inquire about having Sherese speak at your event)

Podcast: https://healandsell.buzzsprout.com

Instagram: https://www.instagram.com/thebizdoula

Tik Tok: https://www.tiktok.com/@thebizdoula

Facebook: https://www.facebook.com/thebizdoula

PART ONE:

THINGS I WISHED I'D KNOWN

CHAPTER 1

I GOT A BIG EGO

"I talk like this 'cause I can back it up."
—Beyonce

It was the summer of 2009, and Beyonce dropped her third single, "Ego," from her album *I Am . . . Sasha Fierce*. The song was perfectly suited for the album concept as Beyonce introduced us all to her alter ego, Sasha Fierce. And at the time, it was perfectly suited for me. I was in the process of getting a divorce, understanding my new identity, and embracing my womanhood and newfound independence. As a symbol of this independence, I purchased a 2005 Black GT Mustang convertible and boy, was she bad (the car and I). I remember riding with the top down, the wind blowing in my hair with the California sunshine on my face, as I blasted this song while truly feeling myself.

"Feeling myself" was a phrase I had heard so many times, and it accurately captured the moment. I knew what I wanted, wasn't afraid to speak my mind, and exuded confidence. But what does it mean and where did the idea of an alter ego come from? Popular phrases of "feeling myself" or someone being on an "ego trip" have their roots in the work of one psychologist, Sigmund Freud.

We can attribute songs about egos and popular phrases about the ego to Sigmund Freud's early work on the development of personality structures. Freud described the structure of personality in three parts: the id, the ego, and the superego. Although his theory of personalities is somewhat outdated, we can use these terms to describe our internal conflict. It is like the theoretical devil and angel on your shoulder influencing your daily decisions. The conflict unfolds in our consciousness (the ego) where our desires (the id) and our morality (the superego) contend.

THE ID

The id holds the seat of our most primal desires. To some degree, it can feel like it operates in a childlike and impulsive fashion. It wants what it wants, and it wants it right now. The id seeks fulfillment and doesn't really care about the consequences nor does it adhere to reason. Let's look at an example of how this works.

Let's say you're scrolling on social media and an ad pops up for some cute summer sandals. You click on the ad and it takes you to the website to purchase the sandals for $79. You don't really need another pair of sandals; in fact, you already have a couple of pairs in your closet that are the same color as the ones you want to buy. Besides that, you know these shoes would put you beyond your budget for the month, but you decide that having these shoes is more important than your budget and you purchase them anyway. This is how the id works.

This example also demonstrates another concept, the pleasure principle. In most of the decisions we make, this principle is in effect as we are either moving closer to pleasure or away from pain.

THE SUPEREGO

The superego is like the counterbalance to the id. While the id operates from desire with no regard for consequences, the superego is concerned with right and wrong and is not concerned with reality. The superego may often come up with the ideal or perfect response to a situation, even though it may not be practical.

However, the concept of what is considered "ideal" is normally taught to us as children through our culture, society, guardians, and parents. Simply put, the superego represents your conscience and provides rewards or punishments for overcoming or giving into the id. Let's go back to our sandal example above and determine what role the superego plays in our decision making process.

As you're looking at those cute summer sandals, envisioning how they'll be the perfect accent to your outfit, the superego may step in and remind you that you've already hit your clothes and shoe budget for the month, so your shoe purchase wouldn't be wise right now. However, you ignored your superego and purchased them anyway. You entered your information and hit the "buy button" to complete your purchase. Suddenly, you feel different.

During the buying experience, you were excited to buy the shoes; you told yourself you deserved them, you had a long week, or that you hadn't bought any shoes in three months so this was justified, and the feeling remained until you clicked "Buy." Boom! Buyer's remorse kicks in, and you're experiencing a feeling of regret or guilt from your purchase. This feeling of guilt and regret for giving into the id comes from the superego. The superego reminds you that you failed to meet your goal, and some sort of mental punishment ensues.

THE EGO

The ego strives to balance between the id and the superego.

This is the conscious connection that balances reality with our desires and morality and then takes action. The word "ego" that we often hear in songs or in descriptions of celebrities and politicians is an overall description of the entirety of self, the whole person. So let's pick up from our last example and see what role the ego plays in this. You're back scrolling on social media and see an ad for a pair of shoes you like and click on the link to see how much they cost. The shoes are $79, and you know they are outside of your budget, so the ego might make some other suggestions to satisfy the id and the superego.

Instead, you may realize that in two weeks your clothing budget will be replenished at the beginning of the month. You decide to save the link to the shoes and delay the purchase until your budget is reset. Another option might be your ego listens to your id's desire to buy the shoes, but compromises and decides you'll only spend half the amount on a pair of sandals at $39. In this way, you also satisfy your superego. You didn't quite blow your budget, and you still get a cute pair of sandals, even though they weren't the exact pair that you originally desired. This compromise is the internal conflict that plays a role in everyday situations.

Being aware of our internal processes puts us in the driver's seat in emotion regulation and is the first part of the challenge to lead with our emotions. If we are not self-aware, we can make decisions blindly and only interpret our choices as bad or good when we review the aftermath of our decision.

Instead, we need to recognize that our ego can influence our thoughts, behaviors, and emotions and is a key concept to understand the pieces at play. Now that we have a clear understanding of the id, the superego, and the ego, we see that the ego is neither bad nor good, but the components of the ego and the experiences that shaped us determine how we choose to interpret the world and make decisions.

THE ROLE OF CHILDHOOD

The id and superego are shaped and fashioned rather quickly from childhood, most specifically by our parents, guardians, teachers, coaches, and the like. As infants, we rely on our parents for our basic needs like food, clothes, and shelter. Beyond the basics, there are so many schools of thought on proper parenting that even within the same household, as many older siblings can attest, children were not raised the same. Maybe your parents subscribed to the idea that you should be held closely, not allowed to cry much, and maybe even let you sleep in their bed. Or you could have had a parent that didn't cater to your every beck and call and believed that letting you cry it out and spending time alone in your playpen would make you a more mature child. Because we were so young, most of us don't remember how we were treated as infants and don't realize how it plays a role in how we respond today.

Scientists suggest that there are harmful implications to letting your child cry it out versus comforting them or meeting their needs. In fact, in the primary months of infancy, the child learns trust, self-regulation, and how to adapt to stress. The first year of life is a critical period to establish trust with the world, the caregiver, and the world of self. When the baby's needs are met, the child can see their environment and the world as supportive and trustworthy.

However, when the child's needs are not met and dismissed, the baby will see the world as unsupportive and have a sense of mistrust in relationships and their self-confidence will be undermined. As the child continues to grow, they will feel a need to find ways to fill the inner emptiness. In addition to establishing trust, how we're raised as infants also impacts our ability to self-regulate our emotions.

Emotional self-regulation is the ability to adapt and manage our behaviors, emotions, and thoughts in a socially acceptable way that supports our long-term goals. In short, it's the way we manage stressors and how we calm ourselves down when we feel upset and cheer ourselves up when we're feeling down. Our introduction to developing these skills came from our treatment as infants. The baby learns how to self-regulate based on the treatment from the parents. When the baby's needs are met without long-term distress, it primes the baby for calmness. Similarly, when the baby gets scared and the parent holds and comforts them, the baby learns what is soothing and that gets integrated into their ability to self-regulate. If a baby does not experience calmness and soothing through the care of the parents, how will the baby learn to do it on its own? Instead, the baby will learn how to shut down when experiencing distress, stop feeling, and stop trusting.

In addition to shutting down when experiencing distress, consistent dismissal, and ignoring their needs, the baby's body begins to prime itself for the long-term stress response. This long-term stress response actually affects the nervous system in the child's body and can be related to irritable bowel syndrome and other digestive issues. Early childhood stress is toxic to lifelong health.

LIMITING BELIEFS

When we are young, the superego is developed as guardians, caregivers, parents, teachers, media, and society made an impression on our brain of what is considered good and acceptable. So often, the superego is crafted by the culture and the environment that we grow in. Thus, a lot of our limiting beliefs about ourselves, about the world, about those around us came from those that had input in on our superego.

A limiting belief is an idea, thought, or conviction that you believe to be true that negatively impacts your interactions with yourself and those around you. This belief is usually coupled with some sense of emotional or spiritual sense of certainty. This belief, fueled by your emotions, has an overwhelming power to manifest in your life. In short, it can direct or limit the actions you take, hijack or harness your passion, skew your perspective, shape your character, and define what you believe to be real, true, or possible for yourself.

Our limiting beliefs are harbored in our thoughts and become very powerful because they can control our emotions, which lead to our behaviors that impact how we act and react to life's situations. What we believe about ourselves can be the number one tool to support our dreams or lead us to failure. I'm sure you've heard the saying, "If you believe you can or you can't, you're right." This phrase highlights the importance of our beliefs in our actions. Think about some limiting beliefs that you may have said to yourself in the past: I'm not good at speaking to an audience of people. If I could've lost ten pounds, he may have dated me. Bad things always happen to me. There aren't any more good men left. I could never start my own business.

I'm sure you probably have good reasons for believing these things, mainly because your limiting beliefs come from assumptions you made about your life experiences. As humans, we tend to allow a painful experience to blanket our interpretation of the world as a whole and use it as a means to simplify and guide us through life. One of the dangerous things about limiting beliefs is that they are self-validating and self-fulfilling, meaning we will attract circumstances and situations that will reinforce our beliefs. This is why we can see themes, patterns, and repeating cycles throughout our life. Here are a few common limiting beliefs to identify in your life (this list is not meant to be inclusive, but it's a starting point):

- I am not worthy.

- I am not pretty, etc.).

- I do not deserve the etc.). enough (insert good, skinny, smart, rich, (promotion, house, career,

- I am unable to be loved or I am unlovable as I am.

- I don't have enough ____(support, money, time, experience, etc.).

Your limiting beliefs shape how you view your money, your career, your age, your race, and your relationships. They can determine how far you will go in life or how successful or unsuccessful you will be. In some instances, it's helpful to unpack and analyze who had a hand in creating the morality side of your psyche and figure out what beliefs should belong there and which ones should not belong there.

For example, you may have been given advice that you may not have understood at the time and just accepted. Although it may have been helpful in the moment to keep you from experiencing pain or harm, like someone correcting you for proudly sharing your accomplishment because it was arrogant, rude, or selfish, it could hurt your confidence in the long run. Comments like that might actually teach you that in order to be accepted, you must shrink yourself for others. That type of thinking will reduce your self-confidence and cause you to believe that unless you act this way with others, they will not like or accept you for who you are. Over time this conditioning of your young mind can make you play small and safe and stay mediocre.

Another area where limiting beliefs greatly impact our adulthood is in our beliefs about money. Some of us may have grown up believing that struggling financially was the only way to get through in the world and that abundance wasn't our lot in life. Or you may have grown up believing that financial resources were always scarce, so you have to save and reject ideas of enjoyment or pleasure. Even further, some of us grew up believing that money was evil and anyone that had money was seen as a greedy and deplorable person, so the only way to truly live life was to live frugally. Now don't get me wrong. I'm all for budgeting, living within your means, and getting out of debt, but my limiting beliefs about money and struggle kept me in debt.

I wholeheartedly believed that struggle was normal. Struggling to pay rent, poor credit, an overdrafted bank account, having utilities cut off, cars repossessed—all of that was normal. I thought everyone that didn't live that life was an anomaly. The funny thing is I used to tell myself that it would get better after I moved out on my own, got a degree, and found a good-paying job. But all those problems continued to follow me from city to city, job to job, and it didn't matter how much more I earned.

Why? Because I inherently believed that struggle was normal, I would find a way to put myself in severe financial stress, whether that was giving money to help other people or just living above my means. Eventually, I realized that the money wasn't the issue, but it was my limiting belief around its ability to flow to me and my acceptance of a life of struggle. These beliefs were subconsciously handed down to me, and I was unaware that it had even happened. I had to break that cycle and find a way out.

At first, I started reading books like *The Millionaire Next Door*, *The Richest Man in Babylon*, and *Rich Dad, Poor Dad* to help me understand how to use money better. I tried the techniques, made the budgets, and tried saving the money, but it only lasted for a little while, then I would find myself right back where I was again. It wasn't until I read *Think and Grow Rich* by Napoleon Hill that I realized my thoughts, beliefs, and emotions played a heavy unseen role in how I used money.

I turned to any thought leaders that were discussing money and limiting beliefs. I had to consume as much information as I could to help me remove the subconscious blocks I had against receiving more, creating abundance, and living a fulfilled life that didn't include living paycheck to paycheck. While it has been helpful to understand some limiting beliefs that were developed in childhood and at other times, it's just as helpful to identify the limiting belief as they exist right now in my life. You get to determine how far back you need to go or whether to deal with the impact of the limiting belief in the current moment. It's not a one-size-fits-all approach.

HOW TO CLEAR LIMITING BELIEFS

Whether you are dealing with limiting beliefs around money, relationships, career, business, or other areas of your life, I've found that this three-step approach helps me identify subconscious limiting beliefs.

The first step is to cultivate awareness. The hardest part about identifying limiting beliefs is that they are a part of our psyche; therefore, we believe they are inherently true and a part of our belief system. I've worked through limiting beliefs about myself, relationships, money—you name it. Every time I think I've gotten them all cleared out, lo and behold, I identify another one. Limiting beliefs are weaved into the fabric of who we are. You won't find them all overnight, and the key is to be patient with yourself and show compassion. As you challenge yourself to cultivate awareness, you can begin to identify the limiting beliefs. One way I cultivate awareness is by paying attention to resistance.

My definition of resistance is any negative energy (thoughts, emotions, behaviors) that arise when we want to make a change for the better that will challenge us. Sometimes resistance will look like procrastination, fear, self-sabotage, perfectionism, etc.

Cultivating awareness to your particular patterns of resistance will help you notice your limiting beliefs. Resistance only arises to reinforce and protect what you already believe to be true. It's an attempt to keep you in your comfort zone.

To identify some of your limiting beliefs, start with the list given in the last section. Did any of those limiting beliefs resonate with you?

Once you've become aware of a limiting belief, it's time to reframe it. But the only way we can reframe a belief is by discovering the truth behind it. This may sound hard, but one way to turn your limiting belief on its head is to look at it objectively. Take some time to look at the limiting belief with a deeper examination and determine if you actually have evidence to the contrary.

Limiting beliefs are attached to language like, "I'll never be able to," "Nothing ever works out for me," or "This always happens to me." Using words like *never*, *nothing*, and *always* tend to frame our beliefs in absolute terms as if the words sometimes and occasionally don't exist. Your issues don't "always happen to you," so look for evidence on the contrary. The point here is to expand your thoughts and vision to see outside of the limited view your mind created, grasp and see the abundant truth around you, and realize that life is conspiring for your success.

I had a client who used to believe that no matter what, she would always struggle with money. She grew up believing there was never enough to go around, a belief that was passed down from her family. No matter the job, she always struggled to stay afloat.

Every time she had a good amount saved, something major would happen that required her to spend the money and put her back in cycles of debt. Once she identified the limiting belief, I helped her reframe and rewire her beliefs around money. She was able to go from struggling to getting by to expanding her side business from just $75 a month to $2,000 a month.

The last step in the process is to practice gratefulness. A lot of our limiting beliefs are centered around inadequacy, lack, and scarcity, and having a practice that shifts you into a mindset of abundance will make a huge impact in the long run. Having a gratitude practice can strengthen your mental health and amplify positive emotions, as well as attract more abundance into your life.

Remember what you focus on in your life will expand. We have a choice to focus on limiting beliefs and expand those or focus on abundance and expand its impact in our life. Instead of looking at new opportunities as a possibility to fail and be rejected, we can first be grateful for the new opportunities and the chance to grow and learn something new.

POINTS TO PONDER

We're all aware of our primal desires of the id and how we should curb them, but I want to encourage you to take a look at the superego. We have the task, as we go through adulthood, to not just fully and wholeheartedly accept whatever is in the superego, but we need to filter out what belongs here and what doesn't. Determine where your inner critic is coming from and identify those limiting beliefs that keep you playing small in life.

CHAPTER 2

WHAT U WORKIN' WITH?

"Sorry, I missed your call. I was staring at the screen wondering why on earth you couldn't just text me."

Spoken like a true introvert! I won't say how many times I've ended phone conversations thinking the exact same thing. I prefer text messages over FaceTime, intimate groups over crowded parties, and I appreciate solitude. I was quick to embrace online shopping (Oh, the joy of ditching overcrowded stores) and was extremely grateful when my job went 100 percent virtual. Who would've thought life could be so good? But where did we get the categories of introvert or extrovert, the four temperaments, or even the Myers-Briggs assessment? What does it all mean? If you're like me, you've taken your fair share of personality tests to discover who you are and what makes you tick. Let's go back to Ancient Greece where this all began and determine how this impacts your emotions today.

Hippocrates, sometime between 460-370 BC, developed the theory of the four temperaments. This was the first written theory between health and personality that we know today. Hippocrates, and later Galen, believed that your personality/temperament was based on the dominance of various fluids or "humors" in the body. The temperament theory suggests that the imbalance of four bodily fluids—blood, phlegm, black bile, and yellow bile—impact your health, personality, and behavior. An excess of one of the humors in your body was responsible for the temperament that you displayed. An excess of blood produced a more cheerful, Sanguine temperament. An excess of phlegm in the body produced a calm, Phlegmatic temperament. Too much black bile caused the depressive, Melancholic temperament. And an excess in yellow bile humor was believed to produce an angry, Choleric temperament.

Although scientists have refuted the existence of humors impacting the body in that fashion, psychologists still recognize the four primary temperament types: Sanguine, Phlegmatic, Melancholic, and Choleric. You can have a primary and secondary temperament type. The four temperaments are the foundation for the development of the Myers-Briggs Type Indicator (MTBI) personality test that most of us have probably taken in school or at work at some point in our lives. The difference in the MTBI is that it expands and combines the four temperament types and creates sixteen personality types. For the sake of our discussion, we're reviewing it on a simpler level and focusing on the primary four temperament types.

SANGUINE

A Sanguine usually has a hearty and energetic temperament and is a social extrovert. They are usually extremely people- oriented as they are social and talkative and find social interactions invigorating. Being surrounded by people energizes them, and they're usually not picky about whom they get to know. As such, Sanguines usually have a lot of charisma and often easily attract attention, allowing them to make friends quickly and enjoy having conversations with new people. You may find that your Sanguine friends like to convince people to come along and hang out and encourage people to work together.

Characteristics

The Sanguine temperament is the most versatile amongst the temperaments. Sanguines usually have a wide range of emotions and behaviors. They are an optimistic type of person who believes life is exciting and fun-filled and should be lived to the fullest. A lack of engagement or activity can cause them stress because they enjoy living their life in a high-energy format. Their attention span is usually directly related to how much they are enjoying the conversation or what they are doing. Here are some additional details behind their strengths and, in extreme moments, how their weaknesses will be exhibited:

Emotional Strengths	Emotional Weaknesses
Expressive	Exaggerates or embellishes
Enthusiastic	Restless energy
Great speaker	Egotistical
Lives in the present	Controlled by circumstances
Spontaneous	Forgetful or disorganized
Welcoming	Fears rejection
Great adapters	Poor concentration
Optimist	Trouble completing what was started
Leader	Self-absorbed
Forgives quickly	Avoids conflicts

PHLEGMATIC

While the Sanguine temperament is the most common, Phlegmatic is also common and can be viewed as the opposite of the Sanguine temperament. Phlegmatics have a balanced temperament and are usually service oriented. They are usually reliable, responsible, devoted, and can sometimes be workaholics. Because they are task-oriented, they usually have a great capacity for work that requires precision and accuracy but expends minimal amounts of energy.

Characteristics

The Phlegmatic is an introvert who is usually slow-paced and passive. This can cause a lack of ambition or sense of urgency when working or dealing with time-sensitive decisions. They usually maintain a calm demeanor and speak quietly but clearly, with noticeable pauses that sometimes lack emotion or intonational leaps. Phlegmatics are able to handle stressful situations more easily than the other temperaments. But in cases where emotions are running high, they can shut down or turn off and stop reacting completely.

Emotional Strengths	Emotional Weaknesses
Low-key	Unenthusiastic
Sympathetic	Too Compromising
Easy going / relaxed	Fearful and worried
Quiet, but witty	Too shy
Patient	Indecisive
Conservative	Avoids change
Introspective	Antisocial
Stable	Risk-averse
Attentive	Brutally honest
Rational	Apathetic

MELANCHOLIC

We are all familiar with the word melancholy, but this temperament isn't describing someone who we would consider depressed.

The Melancholic temperament is a perfectionist introvert who lives in caution. They have high sensitivity, emotionality, anxiety, and good creative abilities. Because they are idealists who like to have things a particular way and are quality oriented, they pay attention to detail. Melancholic people tend to also be high-guilt individuals that analyze and worry about how things could have been handled differently. They find it hard to live completely in the present.

Characteristics

Melancholic temperaments tend to be emotionally protective and guarded. They usually resist communicating their feelings for that reason. They usually follow the rules, and in unfamiliar environments, they will be cautious and attentive. Although they are usually private about their feelings, they tend to have a very sensitive emotional nature; feelings dominate their being. They can be deeply moved by beauty or distress. Because of their perfectionist tendencies, they do not do well with criticism and can be easily hurt. Only praise can motivate a Melancholic.

This temperament is factual, logical, and analytical. They plan and ponder before they act and will not engage in impulsive behavior. On one end of the spectrum, if a Melancholic is not allowed to plan in advance, it can cause distress for them. On the opposite end of the spectrum, it should be noted that they have a beautiful imagination, well-developed intuition, and are highly resourceful. Many artists, writers, sculptors, musicians, and other creative people are Melancholics. They draw their energy from their new creations. The Melancholic temperament is the rarest of the four types.

Emotional Strengths	Emotional Weaknesses
Creative	Overly sensitive
Thoughtful	Highly critical
Empathetic	Low self-esteem
Self-sacrificing	Holds grudges

Purposeful	Perfectionist
Analytical	Overthinker
Genius tendency	Easily offended
Intuitive	Skeptical
Attentive	Phobia prone
Loyal	Stubborn

CHOLERIC

Cholerics tend to be identified as the most powerful temperament. Exhibiting a high level of extroversion, they may be considered the alphas of our society. They exude confidence and are independent and strong willed. They are brief and direct, which can sometimes come off as rudeness. They seek to be in control of situations and are usually leaders and directors.

Characteristics

The Choleric is characterized by the desire to dominate and exert powerful energy but sometimes have weak self-control. They tend to face opposition head-on with the intention of getting results. Cholerics are driven to succeed and can be seen as domineering, opinionated, and somewhat controlling in relationships. They tend to enjoy competition and do not like to lose. They believe in proving oneself.

Emotional Strengths	Emotional Weaknesses
Leader	Controlling
Must correct wrongs	Self-righteous
Independent	Inflexible
Exudes confidence	Unsympathetic (dislikes tears & emotions)

Energetic	Impatient
Goal-oriented	Workaholic
Charisma	Mood swings
Persistent	Hasty
High self-esteem	Extremely competitive
Dynamic	Quick-tempered
Compulsive need for change	Unable to relax

CAN TEMPERAMENTS CHANGE?

To prepare for this chapter, I thought it would be wise to retake the temperament test and discuss my temperament with you all and explain how it has affected my life. Well, to my surprise, I took the test and received a different temperament result from when I took the test five years ago. I thought something must be wrong, so I took it again. I ended up taking the test five times and it came out with the same answer. I sat there wondering how this was possible. How could this be? Your temperament is supposed to remain pretty consistent throughout your life, at least that's what most studies say.

Then it dawned on me. In the last five years, I've gone to therapy and done a lot of deep emotional and spiritual work to heal old wounds and trauma. The temperament that I received previously may have been a shield or cover of some sort that I used to protect myself. I laugh when I say this, but my primary temperament was Choleric and my secondary temperament was Melancholic. I was a real tyrant. I don't know how my family, friends, or significant others even handled me.

My demanding tone, desire to control, and quick temper were something to behold. Of course, I had some good traits too: I protected those I didn't feel could protect themselves. I would stand up to bullies as a child (and even in the workplace). I was dependable and not easily discouraged when given a task. But all of that was truly armor, and I didn't realize this until I tested a few days ago and my result was Sanguine. Sanguine? Me, Sherese, a Sanguine? No way.

I started replaying old stories that I had convinced myself were true. I'm not really interested in being social, and I feel better when I can recharge alone. But when I took a serious inventory of my actual activities, I realized that I may have always been a suppressed Sanguine. Hilarious, I know. I immediately recalled stories of my young childhood from my mom and grandparents about how friendly I was as a child. I used to speak to strangers on the street, smiling and waving. I invited everyone to be my friend or come to my house and play.

Then life happened, and I watched my mom (who in retrospect operated as a Sanguine) get taken advantage of and taken for granted. From those experiences, although I never made this a conscious decision, I vowed to not let people do that to me. When we experience trauma, we often become who we need to be just to survive. So I morphed into a Choleric. I'm the boss and I control the situation and no one will take advantage of me. It suited me for a very long time; I remember instances of morphing my temperament as early as fifth grade (where I was the bully to the bully) and probably as late as my early thirties. We're talking decades of wearing a shield. My journey through emotional healing helped lift the weight of the shield off of me, and I was able to naturally revert back to my pre-trauma temperament as a Sanguine.

POINTS TO PONDER

Why is all this important to my emotional state? Knowing my weaknesses and strengths of my particular emotional temperament helped me build stronger relationships and navigate life's circumstances better. Operating blindly can lead us to endless cycles and patterns with unwanted results. The more you know about yourself, the more you're able to craft the life you truly desire.

In addition, as you do the work to take back control of your emotional state, you may find that old, familiar, comfortable traits and habits fall off of you. Yes, sometimes my Choleric urges still pop up, but I already recognize it as a defense mechanism.

Awareness is the first key to discovering and healing your old emotional wounds. Don't be alarmed if you find that your temperament, your energy, and your desires start to change.

CHAPTER 3

I'M EMOTIONAL AND I CAN'T LET GO

"We all live at the mercy of our emotions. Our emotions influence and shape our desires, thoughts and behaviors and above all our destiny."
—Dr. T.P. Chia

In the early 2000s, Carl Thomas released an album entitled *Emotional*, and one of the biggest hits from that album was a song of the same name. If you haven't heard it in a while, do yourself a favor and listen to that song. He was all in his feelings, working through the termination of his relationship and battling the reasoning and emotions that came along with it. It was the song of all songs for every breakup that anyone experienced in that season. It's the typical breakup pattern, which is why I believe the song was so popular. We struggle to let go of those we have emotionally attached ourselves to, even after logical reasons and explanations. Such was my plight in 2002.

I had been dating this guy since my freshman year in college. He was fun, goofy, sensitive, caring, and spoiled me. From my perspective, we adored each other; had grand ideas of love, marriage, and family; and had a we-can-accomplish-anything- together type attitude. I was barely eighteen and met him while I was still living in Chicago with my father and stepmother. You know, that young puppy-love type experience. In this time period, he helped me through some of the most painful experiences in my life. I ended up running away from home and reaching out to him in this poorly planned out exit. He and his family let me stay with them for a bit while I figured things out.

For the previous six years, I had been estranged from my family that had raised me. I hadn't seen or been allowed to speak to my mom, my stepdad (who I call Dad), my brother, and my little sister who all lived in California, nor my grandparents (or aunts, uncles, or cousins) that lived in Chicago. So when I ran away from home and had no place to go, he and his family helped me reconcile with my estranged family members. I moved back with my grandparents to finish out one more year of school and then decided I finally wanted to go back home to California.

I didn't know what our relationship would look like for us, but all I knew is that I didn't want to be separated from him; I didn't think I could handle it since I had already experienced the devastation of being separated from my loved ones before. So I tried to convince him to come with me and move to California where we could start our new life. My family welcomed him, and a close family friend even offered him a place to live for free until he could get on his feet. In my eyes, I knew we could work this out and be together. Well, that didn't work out at all, and we ended up breaking up in a very, very emotional and painful fashion.

I was depressed for months and my anxiety was through the roof as I obsessed over the "what ifs" and "should haves." I was angry with him for being logical and deciding to stay with his family and a strong support system in Chicago. I was confused as to why he felt that finishing his degree in Chicago was the best decision.

And most of all, I was dumbfounded that he wisely chose stability over our fairytale love. "Stability? Stability? At the end of the day, that's what's most important to you? I guess everything you said to me was a lie!" Yup, that's pretty much where my thoughts and emotions were during this entire time. I let my emotions wreak havoc on my mood and my body and I lost so much weight from just not eating enough. The pain of being detached from him was overwhelming. Looking back, I realized that how I responded to our breakup was the same way I responded when my father and stepmother showed up late at night to take custody of me from my grandparents. This triggered an anxiety response of being unable to let go of people from that point forward.

HOW EMOTIONS ARE CREATED

We've been taught that our emotions are created on the whim and in the moment from a specific part of the brain. But in fact, they're created based on a combination of sensory input and predictions from past experiences and similar events. This is powerful because we no longer have to subscribe to the model of believing that we have no control over our emotions and are always at the mercy of how we feel in the moment. Dr. Lisa Feldman Barrett, PhD, a distinguished professor in psychology, wrote extensively about the subject in her book, *How Emotions Are Made*. Her book is based on scientific evidence and testing which I'll attempt to translate into laymen's terms here.

Barrett presents the "theory of constructed emotions" to explain how emotions are made. Our brain creates emotions based on our unique experience in the moment. This explains why when we experience joy we can shout with excitement, cry tears of joy, or sit in awe of the moment. Our brain scans our environment to receive sensory input on how we should respond to the moment and then compares the current situation to past experiences where we've had similar moments of joy. The brain then predicts the appropriate emotional expression for the specific moment. If the prediction was wrong, the brain makes adjustments moving forward. Our emotions are not reactions to the world. We are not passive receivers of input but an active constructor of our emotions. The key fact to note here is that your emotions are not triggered. You create them and you feel what your brain believes.

In addition to using sensory input and past experiences to predict the appropriate emotional response in a specific moment, your bodily resources impact how you feel as well. Barrett uses the term "body budget" to describe this transaction. You can liken the body budget to having a bank account. For every movement of your body, internal or external, the brain calculates how much energy it will take for you to process the moment and makes withdrawals or deposits into your nervous system and other areas.

It can release hormones or reduce certain functions to maximize the energy needed for the moment. For example, I have a friend who is deathly afraid of cats and had a very bad experience with a cat jumping on her back as a child. As the cat slid down her back, it dug its nails into her, which left her in tears, screaming and writhing in pain. Now when we go for a walk, the mere sight of any cat prompts a memory of her childhood experience. Her body determines she needs an increase in energy and releases cortisol to give her a burst so she can run, jump, or flee from the cat.

Her sensory input of the cat causes her brain to remember the fear and anxiety she experienced in her childhood and predicts that her current experience will be a replay of what happened to her as a child. Her body releases cortisol to give her energy, and before I've even seen the cat, my friend screams and runs across the street. All of this happens almost seamlessly, without having full awareness to stop the reaction because her body is trained to respond and help her flee real or perceived danger.

This happens to all of us in various ways. Whether it's a comment about your big forehead, your boyfriend having women as friends, or your manager having longer conversations with your coworker instead of you, we react. In each instance, we construct our emotions based on the thoughts that arise from our analysis of the moment, compare it to past triggering events, and then respond as if that past event is happening in the present moment. Most of us are not even aware that this is happening, so we find ourselves repeating cycles and patterns wondering how it keeps happening.

The key to begin breaking this habit is to practice awareness. To do this, when you first begin to feel these emotions arise, check in with your body. How does your body respond to anxiety, anger, frustration, agitation, or disappointment? For me, if I'm feeling ashamed, I usually get flushed and I can feel my temperature rise, heat coming up the back of my neck, and a tightness in my stomach. I then recognize it as my bodily shame response, and this clues me in to slow down and process my emotions, words, and actions before I take my next step.

If you have time, jot down the emotions you're feeling, be it feeling unworthy, unloved, too vulnerable, and such. After you write down what you're feeling, take some time to breathe and write down some words to counter that feeling. For example, I write down things like, "My worthiness is absolute and cannot change," "It doesn't matter if I make a mistake," or "It's ok to show cracks in my armor." I wasn't created to be superwoman, and as a matter of fact, she does not exist. Continue writing those things down until you've countered all the emotional beliefs that come up in the moment, and then reach out to a friend or confidant and tell them what happened. Shame grows when you don't give it a voice. You will continue hiding, repressing, and trying to fix something or pretend like everything is OK when it really isn't.

YOUR BODY AND YOUR EMOTIONS

Barrett explains that in addition to you constructing your emotions, your body is also assisting you in the response by allocating the resources needed for you to move. In short, your brain applies meaning to every sensation you feel in your life. With each sensation, your body allocates resources, called body budgeting, and plays a vital role in keeping you alive. These resources include what is needed to run your organs, your immune system, and your metabolism. Each of these resources can be replenished or depleted by your eating, drinking, or sleeping habits. Spending time with loved ones, meditation, and even sex can help replenish your energy resources. Your brain has to manage all of the spending and replenishing and predict your energy needs, so it's managed like a body budget. Your body is able to make these predictions and allocate what resources you'll need to respond based on past experiences.

You can think of your body budget in the same way that you operate a car. Every time you turn on the car, you need gas, oil, brake fluid, transmission fluid, a fully charged battery, running lights, and such. Every time you move your car, it is using resources, from shifting gears, to turning, and even while sitting at a stoplight. It knows how much energy to spend to go from 0 to 100, to brake quickly, or make a left-hand turn at 30 mph. Like our bodies, cars need maintenance and their resources replenished in order to function at an optimal level. Our bodies also need the same care to operate and maintain good health.

YOUR CULTURE AND EMOTIONS

Beyond responding to our present moment based on past experiences, Barrett states there's another element at play in the expression of our emotions. These factors are largely based on culture and our beliefs about how to respond to certain emotions. Culture is defined as a deposit of knowledge, values, beliefs, customs, communication, habits, and language that encompasses socially acceptable behavior and norms that people have in common with their environment. This plays a crucial role in our social lives. Culture shapes how we make sense of our work, our identity, and our relationships; it sets parameters for maintaining social order and influences our everyday actions and experiences in society.

For example, I once lived with a roommate who was amazed by my dance skills. Trust me. By no means am I that great, but I do enjoy moving my body. I find it to be one of the precious joys in my life. One day after she complimented me, I shared with her that she doesn't have to be perfect and can just enjoy the sound and allow her body to move.

She responded, "Oh, no. I can't do that. I'd look silly."

I asked, "Well, who's judging you?"

She said, "When I was a kid, if we started dancing, my dad would

say, 'Stop that, you look silly.' So I grew self-conscious and decided I wouldn't try to dance."

This is a key example of culture at play here. Dancing for her brought on feelings of judgment and fear of ridicule because her parents didn't see value in it and thought it was more or less a useless skill. My parents, on the other hand, viewed dancing as normal. They might laugh at some of my moves, but I was never told to stop. So now I dance, whether I look silly or not, and completely enjoy the experience. In my home culture, dancing is acceptable, and in her home culture, not so much.

In the same way, I have a friend that grew up in an impoverished area and a harsh environment. His family worked hard and did what they could to survive. He was the youngest child and basically grew up taking care of himself and was allowed free reign to do as he pleased. He saw a lot of his friends die at a young age from gang shootings, street violence, and drug deals gone bad. In this environment, he wasn't allowed to show any emotions at all and he grew numb to the constant daily trauma. Over time, he learned that men in his culture only accepted the expression of one emotion— and that was anger. Any other expression was considered weak: you don't cry; you don't express your disappointments; you have to be consistently ready for war. It wasn't until he got out of that environment that he learned that expressing emotions was OK and that seeking therapy for this trauma was needed as part of his healing.

POINTS TO PONDER

Through understanding that our emotions are not random triggers but constructed by our past experiences, cultural norms, and impacted by our body budget, we're able to see that we are the conscious creators of our reality. We choose the lens through which we will view the world and how we will react to it. Emotions give us meaning, clues to underlying needs, desires, and expectations. We only need to learn how to interpret them correctly. I want you to value your emotions rather than reject them and disdain them. The emotions you've learned to construct are valid, and your brain deemed them crucial because they were most effective in the goal of keeping you alive and thriving in your environment. They were fashioned in the best way possible, and although some may be unorthodox or imperfect, they were necessary for your survival.

The key here is that you've gained awareness and understanding of how your reality is constructed and how your emotions are created. The purpose of this book isn't for you to now deconstruct every emotional response you deem unhealthy, but rather for you to learn how to interpret those emotions and repurpose them to better suit the outcomes you desire based on the truths you've learned about yourself and your overall goals. On your journey through personal growth, you'll have the chance to expose yourself to new concepts, learn ways to process those ideas, and put them into action. You are not 100 percent responsible for what happened to you, but you are 100 percent responsible for how you let it affect your growth right now.

Developing an understanding of your emotional makeup, body budget, and how to process your emotions will change how you react, help you destress your life, end toxic relationships, set better boundaries, live from a place of joy, and make better decisions. This will be a big game changer for your life, so the sooner you learn this, the better. Otherwise, you'll spend countless years like me repeating cycles that you desperately desire to be free from. I've had my fair share of relationships that should have ended sooner than they did, but because I was afraid of feeling the pain of the separation, I held on too long. If you can identify areas in your life to recognize unhealthy repeating cycles, you're already on the road to transformation.

CHAPTER 4

SELF-LOVE, SELF-CARE ... AF

"Self-care is how you take your power back."
—Lalah Delia

Two things are better when not spread too thin: yourself and peanut butter. I've had countless conversations with women all over the world, and many of them struggle with pretty much the same thing—neglecting themselves to take care of others. We are natural nurturers and caregivers, so the tendency to overextend ourselves for the convenience of others almost seems normal. This has been me. For the majority of my life, I've given more than I should have, like taking on debt for others. I've helped people move that wouldn't return the favor when I needed it. I've thrown celebrations for selfish people. I've volunteered time I didn't have to give, which led me to the point of exhaustion. I've loaned money knowing that it would probably not be repaid. More painfully, I've given my heart to someone who trampled on it. And yet, no matter how bad it got, I persisted in overextending myself. This chapter is for you, my dear sweet sister. We're going to cover what I've coined the emotional wellness Achievement Framework (AF).

WHAT IS SELF-CARE

What is self-care really? Feels like it's a fuzzy word, and depending on who you talk to, it could be anything from a girls' night out to booking a therapy session. Honestly, I think it's something that we've ignored and neglected for so long that it is kind of hard for us to define. Simply put, it's a self-initiated restorative practice. It's what you choose to do to replenish and restore your mind, body, soul, and spirit. Since we are all uniquely created, your idea of a restorative self-care practice might be completely different than mine. The point is to make it exactly that: a practice. Having a self-care day, after months or years of burn out, will not be as effective as creating daily, weekly, or monthly practices.

This wasn't the case for me five years ago. I struggled with feeling guilty for allowing myself to take a break, so I often kept my calendar full of things to do from morning to night. The only time I thought it was OK to rest was during my one-week vacation . . . once a year. One week is all that I thought it took to correct 358 days of stress. Without knowing it, I stayed on the brink of exhaustion thinking it was the way things were supposed to be, just a normal part of life. As a result, the health issues kept popping up, like severe asthma, migraines, year-round allergies, ear infections, and more.

My body operated in a state of high stress from continuously overextending myself. It wasn't until I started to let go of some of that stress that I realized that it was impacting my health. I began by implementing a morning ritual that consisted of prayer and reading my Bible. That eventually expanded into meditation, free writing, reading my Bible, affirmations, and ten to fifteen minutes of body movement every morning. I also incorporate one day of rest a week, where I only do things that replenish me spiritually and physically. I usually spend time with family, attend church, work in the garden, read, lounge, or just rest without any requirements or judgments on my productivity.

Here's some truth that might not feel really good when I say it, but just take a moment to really let it sink in before you reject it: the reason we continue to overextend ourselves to the point of exhaustion is that we value other people more than we value ourselves. I know . . . breathe. That can be a lot to absorb. Honestly, though, that's the truth of the matter. Not only do we overextend ourselves for that reason but we are also getting something out of this exchange that we subconsciously need. We feel needed, we appreciate being wanted and desired, and we like coming to the rescue. We are the hero. Again, this may not be something we're willing to admit upfront, but it's definitely in the subconscious mind. Consciously, you might complain about not being able to take a break or feeling like there's always a fire for you to put out. At the end of the day, you are still receiving an emotional benefit and the transaction is rewarding for you whether or not you are consciously aware of it.

We can't blame other people for needing us when we are equally participating in the codependent relationship. Let me give you some more truth here: You are not Jesus junior. You cannot save everyone and everything, and in fact, you weren't built for it either. You have to focus on yourself and what your mind, body, and emotions need for you to be able to help others. Whenever we live in an overextended state, our body believes we are in constant stress and we induce the flight-or-fight response. That response was only supposed to be used in an emergency situation, but now our whole life has turned into one big ongoing emergency.

When you don't take time for self-care, you open yourself up to chronic health issues, increased weight gain or severe weight loss, hair loss, irregular sleep patterns, inflammation in the gut, and a whole host of other things that seem completely unrelated to overextending yourself. If you're reading this and feel like this resonates with you, I want you to know that you do not have to continue in this pattern. For the sake of yourself, your loved ones, family, and friends, it's time to end this cycle.

MY WORTHINESS IS ABSOLUTE

The first thing you need to know is that your worthiness is absolute. If you don't say yes to another request, don't cook another meal, and don't lend another dollar, you are still worthy of love and you are valued. Your worthiness is not up for negotiation, but that's how we treat it when we feel like we have to do all these things for other people. Your worth is not connected to any transactional value. Your worth is inherent. It just is. You must get a firm grasp on this principle before you attempt to do anything else I discuss in this chapter. You are worthy. Your value does not increase or decrease based on what you give. And since we're on the subject, let's also add productivity to this list. Your self-worth is not connected to how much you can produce, create, or finish. Release yourself from measuring your worth by accomplishments.

This is where self-love comes in. I used to think if you were alive, then you obviously knew how to love yourself. If you asked the people around you if they loved themselves, they would admittedly say yes. If you ask them to list examples of how they've demonstrated how they loved themselves, some may be at a loss for words. That was me. You see, I used to believe it was an inherent characteristic of every person to love themself. But as I began to unpack my own hang-ups, I quickly realized that I wasn't actually doing things to show myself love. There's an old saying that goes something like this, "To know and not do, is still not to know." For instance, if you were in a relationship and your boyfriend told you that he loved you but he rarely called to check on you, spent time with you sporadically and only when it was convenient for him, talked down to you, put you in compromising situations, embarrassed you in front of his friends, what does that say about him? After a while, you'd understand that he may say he loves you but doesn't know how to treat someone he loves.

We do the same thing to ourselves. If I say I love myself, but don't get rest, eat poorly, perpetuate negative self-talk, constantly put myself down in front of others even if they're giving me compliments, ignore my health, continuously overextend and deplete myself financially and emotionally for others, would you believe me when I said that I loved myself? Love is not just a word, a feeling, or an emotion. Love is an action word, a verb. I know my parents love me because of all they have given to me. I know my boyfriend loves me because of his consistent investment in our relationship. I know I love myself because my actions demonstrate it. I rest regularly, I diffuse negative self-talk, I make sure I eat healthy food, I'm conscious of my health, and take action to improve my fitness. I give myself grace, I practice forgiveness, and I feed my mind and spirit through uplifting activities. I have boundaries on how I manage my money so I'm not in financial stress. All these things (and many more) demonstrate that I love myself.

IT'S OK TO LET GO

You also need to know that it's OK to let go. I say that because we often overextend ourselves out of fear. Most people usually have a fear of failure and fear of letting themselves or others down. We fear what others might think of us or say about us if we don't live up to their expectations. Somehow, we're a bad mom, daughter, sister, or friend because of one denied request. Serving others for fear you won't receive the love or approval you desire will lead you to burn out. This is especially the case when those you have given to do not return the same level of support and investment that you have given to them. Know that you are enough. Your mere presence is reason enough to be loved. You don't have to complete any further acts to be worthy of love. In some cases, we are in relationships with people that use guilt as a negotiation tool for what they want, playing on our fear of letting others down. Let me say that if you are involved in relationships where this is true, know that guilt is the poor man's currency. In that case, you need to let go of that fear so they can't manipulate you that way.

Doing so is a reflection of the requester's lack of valuable investment or deposits into your love tank that would then cause them to resort to guilt. It's as if they know the request is unreasonable, so in order for the request to be met, they have to use guilt because they missed making current high-value deposits in your life. Recognize this tactic as a red flag and don't allow yourself to fall for it. When guilt has been used in a conversation that requires me to give something, I identify it immediately and speak up. I let the person know that using guilt is not acceptable and will not be used as a tool against me. Whatever I choose to give will be out of the goodness of my heart and this is all. After speaking up as this happens in conversation, exposing the tactic for what it is, and standing my ground that I won't fall for this manipulation, few people try to use guilt as a tactic against me now.

If you're probably nodding your head in agreement while you read this, you know this is something you need to do. But it's easier said than done. Whew! The first time I said no, I felt like the worst person on Earth. It felt icky, it felt awkward, and it felt like it would be a lot easier to just give in and say yes, but I held my ground . . . barely. As soon as I got off the phone, reeling with emotion from my first big no and narrowly escaping being convinced to say yes, I called my friend. This is a friend that I held myself accountable to in regard to my transformation from overextending myself to taking back my life and putting me first. It sounds empowering now, but it all felt so weird and selfish in the moment.

I talked them through what had happened, and then I told them all the reasons and justifications as to why I should say yes. This brave friend stayed on the phone with me to remind me of the repercussions of saying yes, remind me of how overextending myself has affected my health, and remind me that I am worthy no matter what I do or don't do. If it wasn't for my friend, I wouldn't have made it through that season. There were a lot of phone calls and a lot of conversation, but slowly and surely, I began to pull myself out of all the unnecessary commitments to be everybody's hero. It was very slow and it was three years before I truly felt free.

The hardest part of the whole process was letting go of the belief that if I didn't step in and come to the rescue, it would be a disaster financially, physically, and mentally for the people that asked for help. Did some bad things happen because I didn't step in? Yes, but the consequences weren't nearly as severe or as frequent as I thought they would be . . . not even close. So that's my warning to you. As you ease out of this state, your imagination will probably be your worst enemy, but most of the things you imagine about your decision to step back probably won't come true. They will live and you will too. The funny thing is that most people are extremely resourceful and resilient. Where there is a will, they will find a way. In most cases, you actually help remove the crutch of codependency on you, and in the long run, you are helping them become a stronger, more capable adult. As you step into your power, they also step into their power.

BOUNDARIES ARE MY FRIENDS

How did I get to the place of consistently overextending myself and unaware of the cycle I had placed myself in? Well, there are little things called boundaries that I knew nothing about. That wasn't a term I learned in school, nor was it something that I learned in the home. It wasn't until I landed in therapy trying to process my divorce that my therapist mentioned it to me. "Boundaries, what?!" She might as well have been speaking Greek to me. I didn't know that boundaries even existed in relationships. My idea of relationships was to be willing to compromise, sacrifice, and give of yourself until it hurts; 'cause after all, that's what love is, right?

This is probably best demonstrated in the mother and infant relationship. Once the infant is born, the mother shifts her world around and caters to the needs of the child. It doesn't matter if it's day or night, if she's sleep deprived, or drained and confused while trying to adjust to her new role, she is still there for her baby. It isn't until the child develops the mental, emotional, and physical capacity to understand their relationship to the world and their mother that the mother begins to teach them about boundaries.

She teaches her baby how to sit in a chair and eat from a plate, how to use the bathroom rather than a diaper, why it's important to share, and how to manage anger and play well with others. As they develop, she teaches them more boundaries and what's acceptable and unacceptable behavior.

Now, don't get me wrong, I do believe there's a time and place for long-suffering, sacrifice, and compromise, but I don't believe it should be to the point of other people casting you as their savior and being codependent on you. At that point, it has gone too far. That's exactly how my relationship with new boundaries developed over time. The practice of setting my needs before others and respecting my space mentally, spiritually, and physically was a muscle that I needed to develop. Initially, the concept or idea that I could say no if something made me uncomfortable, uneasy, felt draining, depleting, or was inconsiderate didn't even register for me. But I grew stronger with each situation and learned how to set standards that I would not allow others to cross.

I dove into understanding what real boundaries were and how I could use them to help myself and those around me. Let me just say that as I discovered these concepts and began to understand to what degree I was contributing to toxic relationships, it made me angry. You may have heard the saying that the truth will make you free, but first, it will piss you off. That's exactly where I stood as I worked through this process. I was angry about a lot of things, mostly that I allowed it to get this far and that it was deemed normal to be treated that way. I developed a working definition of personal boundaries that has helped me navigate my life and make better decisions. Setting a personal boundary establishes the limits or rules we set for ourselves in our relationship with others to protect their well-being and ours. These personal boundaries can be physical, emotional, financial, or energetic.

The first thing I had to learn about setting personal boundaries is that they help define your sense of self from the other person's needs, feelings, and desires. I often blended the two together in the name of being family, a good friend, or a great team member, but this was detrimental to my personal well-being. As you take inventory of your relationships, note places where the line between your needs, feelings, and desires and theirs are nonexistent or skewed and determine what boundaries need to be set in place to repair the breach. Of course, when you first begin to set boundaries, it will be a shock to all parties involved. The family member, friend, or significant other may become angry by the new standards.

Stand your ground and have a support system in place to help you maintain your new boundaries.

POINTS TO PONDER

- Self-care is an integral piece of your emotional wellness. The framework you can use to achieve it is by first understanding that:
- Your worth is absolute.
- It's important to develop a self-care practice to avoid the burnout- that can be daily, weekly, and monthly.

- Overextending yourself is detrimental to your well-being, and it's important to get comfortable with letting go.
- Personal boundaries are the key to protecting your well-being.

CHAPTER 5

IF YOU'RE HAPPY AND YOU KNOW IT

"Emotions can get in the way or get you on the way." —Mavis Ureke

When I was a little girl, my mom was a preschool teacher at Kindercare. We used to sing, "If You're Happy and You Know It."

That song taught us how to identify the emotion of being happy.

You might clap your hands, you might smile, you might jump, you might run, you might even cry. But have we truly learned how to identify our other emotions? How do you know when you're afraid? How do you know when you're angry? How do you know when you're resentful, agitated, or frustrated? In this chapter, we're going to focus on how to identify your emotions.

At the beginning of the book, we discussed our subconscious and conscious mind. We also discussed the ego's job, which is to protect us. In this case, the mind is concerned with our overall survival, so if we haven't learned how to cope with trauma and deeply painful experiences, the mind will fill in the gap that's necessary for our survival. So to protect us from having a full and complete meltdown and giving up on life at such a very young age, the brain develops defense mechanisms, which help us suppress emotions that don't serve us in the moment.

DEFENSE MECHANISMS

More specifically, a defense mechanism is how we respond to perceived harm or danger that allows the subconscious mind to manage the stress of social situations. Now, while they may serve us in getting through life and surviving, they may not serve us in the long run and may not allow our hearts to heal and to live our best life as an adult.

One reason is they actually hide emotions from our consciousness, which makes it even more complicated and challenging for us to know what we feel. While there are many defense mechanisms, the seven most common ones are denial, compensation, repression, displacement, projection, rationalization, and regression.

Denial

Denial is one of the most common defense mechanisms. The purpose of denial is to blind you from the reality or facts that you don't want to face in order to avoid pain. A person can be in denial about people, places, or things that they find too overwhelming or too emotionally painful to admit to or to deal with. For example, a person who is in a relationship or dating someone who does not show much interest in them, is emotionally unavailable, and only calls them late in the evening to spend time with them, is in denial that the relationship is not a viable one.

They might consider it viable because they are spending time with this person. But that person is denying all the red flags that their partner is displaying in the relationship. It is probably just a convenient hookup.

Compensation

Compensation is another very common defense mechanism.

Compensation is the process by which a person may cover up feelings of inferiority or weakness by overachieving or excelling, which provides them some level of gratification in their life. For example, I dated a guy who felt that he had not achieved what he should have accomplished at his age. As a result, he focused obsessively on getting super fit and working out multiple times a day to create a physique that would allow him to receive a sense of accomplishment, accolades, and acknowledgments for his physical appearance.

Repression

Repression is the subconscious removal of the awareness of painful events or memories in our brains to avoid experiencing them again. However, that doesn't mean that the memories completely dissolve or disappear. Those moments of pain and trauma may unconsciously affect your behavior and your relationships without you really realizing it.

When I was a child, I had to share some distressing information about being physically abused that set off a painful chain of events in my family. Some twenty years later, I was speaking with a family member who asked me if I remembered how the situation unfolded, and I said no. They reminded me that I was the one who spoke up and that started the painful process. My young mind probably repressed the fact that I spoke up because it caused such a monumental fracture in our family that I often regretted saying something.

Displacement

Displacement is a defense mechanism used to avoid emotional pain. It is described as unleashing negative emotions on someone who did not trigger the initial negative reaction. This is often done because getting mad at the real target would cause consequences that the person is unwilling to deal with.

Instead, a person will target someone who is less of a threat to them, and the encounter will result in fewer objections or lower consequences if they fight back. The alternative target might be someone they care for, a work subordinate, or someone they have power over. We can see this demonstrated when a mother comes home from work angry at her manager and she verbally abuses her children and husband.

Projection

Similarly, projection also places a person's internal feelings on another person. When a person has uncomfortable thoughts, feelings, or attributes that they don't want to address, they will assign—or project—those negative qualities to someone else in order to ignore their own uncomfortable feelings. This is illustrated when someone who feels overweight makes fun of someone who they believe to be much larger than themself in order to feel better about themself and avoid handling their own feelings of dislike.

Rationalization

Rationalization is a defense mechanism by which a person may justify why they should not be held accountable or judged because of their behaviors. The person believes they should be excused from judgment for unfounded reasons. An example of this is when a person applies for their dream job and doesn't get it. They may rationalize their disappointment by saying, "It doesn't matter because I heard that the manager was a tyrant anyway."

Regression

Regression is described as a defense mechanism in which a person reverts to an earlier time in their life when they didn't feel as anxious or threatened. The person returns to an earlier stage of development that includes thoughts, feelings, and behaviors of their younger self. In particular, an adult may revert to their childhood defense mechanisms, to a time when those criticisms did not matter and they were safe, to escape the current criticism or pain they're feeling.

PATTERNS TO EXAMINE

Besides defense mechanisms, we need to be aware of other thought patterns or behaviors when examining and identifying our emotions. Most of the time these emotional coping strategies are used unconsciously or unintentionally:

1. **Hyperbole:** This is using exaggeration or absolute statements to overstate a feeling or fact to provoke the listener to understand the importance of the emotion that's being evoked. A person may feel that explaining a situation accurately may not get the response they want, so they exaggerate. People often speak in absolute terms such as, "You never listen to me," "You always ignore me," or "Nothing ever works out for me." The person overstates the facts to gain support or sympathy.

2. **Performance:** A person may connect their self-worth to how much they can produce, create, or finish. Their self-worth is measured by the transactional value of their accomplishments. This person feels the need to be the hero, overachieve, and overextend themselves consistently.

3. **Catastrophizing:** This was a big one for me and is usually connected to fear and anxiety. A person's emotions may be driven by playing out all the worst possible scenarios in order to protect themselves from uncertainty. Fear prevents them from taking calculated risks and often causes them to evoke fear and doubt in others when learning that a friend or loved one wants to take risks, venture out of the norm, or explore an area they are unfamiliar with.

4. **Paranoia:** This person may be on high emotional alert of possible betrayal, attacks, or threats. They often read deeply into someone's words, expressions, or actions and interpret them as intimidation, ultimatums, or imminent harm. This is often done without seeking further clarification and understanding of what was actually intended.

5. **Victim Mentality:** This is an emotional coping strategy used to consistently highlight personal hardships to seek attention or diffuse personal responsibility. It is a state of mind in which a person thinks that life is outside their control and that external forces are out to get them. As a result, they are fueled by pes-

simism, anger, and fear and choose to point fingers and assign blame, believing others are responsible for their unhappiness.

PRIMARY AND SECONDARY EMOTIONS

The Latin definition of the word "emotion" is *emovere*, which means to move out, remove, or agitate. My definition is:

Expression + Motion = Emotion.

Simply put, emotions invite us to express what's going on internally and to take action on those feelings. The problem comes when we're confused about which emotion we are truly feeling and how to interpret the emotion.

In general, when we experience positive emotions, they are meant to reinforce pleasurable experiences and activate the reward systems of the brain, causing us to seek out similar experiences. Negative emotions are meant to tap into our survival instincts to warn us of danger or potential threats. Our response to an event may evoke a primary, secondary, or even a tertiary emotional response. There are 48 recognized emotions and 128 internationally recognized emotions, many of which have no English equivalent. Psychologists generally agree that these emotions should be classified further.

One way to view this is to picture a pyramid divided into layers.

The top layer has the primary emotions such as madness or sadness. The secondary emotions, the middle layer, stem from the primary emotion, and the tertiary emotions stem from the secondary emotions and make up the bottom layer. Primary emotions are broader and are usually visible. Secondary emotions are often caused by the beliefs behind experiencing certain emotions. Tertiary emotions are emotions that are experienced as a result of the secondary emotions. However, there isn't total agreement on which emotions are strictly primary and secondary because each person reacts differently based on how they interpret their thoughts, beliefs, or experiences.

For example, a friend with whom you've been planning a trip calls you last minute to cut back on the number of days on vacation because her boyfriend bought tickets for them to attend a concert during that time. Your first reaction may be anger (primary emotion) because your friend is choosing time with her boyfriend over time with you. This may also lead you to feel disappointment (secondary emotion of sadness) because you won't get to spend as much time with your friend on the trip, and you had great things planned for the two of you. You take some time to process your emotions and find that you are actually insecure (tertiary emotion of sadness) about the future of your friendship because you feel like you're losing your friend.

The problem is that we are constantly processing primary emotions and not processing or addressing the secondary and tertiary emotions. The table created below can help you define the layers of each emotion. However, it's a general guide and is not an absolute structure for emotions.

Sixteen Human Emotions and Their Meaning

Primary	Definition	Secondary	Tertiary
Fear	A distressing emotion that arises from the anticipation of a threat, danger, or pain. It could be mild or paralyzing fear.	Nervousness	Apprehension, distress, worry, anxiety, dread, uneasiness
		Horror	Terror, alarm, horror, panic, fright, mortification, hysteria
Joy	An emotion of great pleasure or delight; a sense of contentment, security, and inner peace. It is	Cheerfulness	Happiness, amusement, euphoria, ecstasy, elation, bliss

	usually caused by something good or exceptionally satisfying.	Enjoyment	Pleasure
		Zest	Enthusiasm, thrill, excitement
Love	An intense emotion of deep interpersonal affection. The foundation of love comes from trust, bonding, and oneness. This emotion can arise with family, friends, and romantic relationships, etc.	Affection	Attraction, sentimentality, fondness, caring, adoration
		Longing	Passion, arousal, obsession, desire, lust, infatuation
Sadness	Sadness can be described as gloom or sorrow. It is a result of experiencing grief, loss, failure, or some type of disadvantage. If this emotion persists in a continued state, it can turn into depression.	Suffering	Agony, anguish, hurt
		Disappointment	Displeasure, dismay
		Neglect	Embarrassment, insecurity, humiliation, alienation, unhappiness
		Sympathy	Pity

		Shame	Guilt, regret, remorse.
Surprise	A feeling of being startled from something unexpected. Surprise can be pleasant, unpleasant, or neutral. Reactions to being surprised will vary from person to person.	Amazement	Astonishment
Anger	Anger is a feeling of strong dislike or displeasure that is characterized by belligerence as a result of feeling wronged. The reaction can be triggered in conflict, embarrassment, injustice, betrayal, or neglect. When experiencing active anger, attacking the target of the anger is likely.	Rage	Resentment, fury, loathing, wrath, hate, bitterness
		Frustration	Exasperation, jealousy
		Irritation	Aggravation, aggression, agitation, torment
		Disgust	Contempt, repulsion

		However, if it's passive anger, it may result in smoldering hostility and tension.		
Acceptance	Acknowledging all the qualities and attributes, both positive and negative, without judging them. It is usually characterized by peace.	Trust	Contentment, happiness
Trust	Firm belief in the dependability, integrity, security, and confidence of someone or something.	Admiration	Acceptance
Anticipation	The emotion of eagerly awaiting something you know is going to happen. It could involve an event, goal, or a person.	Expectation	Interest, optimism, vigilance
Contempt	Although contempt isn't considered one of the primary emotions, it's worth sharing. It's a combination of anger and	Annoyance	Anger, disdain

	disgust.		
Awe	Awe is an emotion composed of reverence, admiration, and fear. Awe can be described as part surprise and part fear.	Distraction	Surprise, amazement
Remorse	An emotion of feeling responsible for wrongdoing that is characterized by sorrow.	Guilt	Disgust, loathing
Disappointment	A feeling of sorrow or dissatisfaction that arises when something you hoped would happen failed to meet expectations or manifest.	Grief	Sadness, pensiveness
Disgust	A feeling of aversion when faced with something offensive.	Offended	Distaste, unpleasant

Resentment	This is a multi-layered emotion of disappointment, fear, and anger.	Bitterness	Depression, agitation
Curiosity	Curiosity is the intrinsic desire to know or see something that is motivated by a desire to gain knowledge.	Diligent	Exploration, learning, investigation

LEAD WITH YOUR EMOTION: THE JOURNEY OF EMOTIONAL SELF-DISCOVERY

When we only see the primary emotions, our actions can seem like they don't make sense. Being able to process our secondary and tertiary emotions will help us understand the hidden factors that govern our reactions. Although your emotions may be hard to decipher, choosing to avoid or suppress them will not help you grow or develop as a person. Not addressing the root causes of your emotions can lead to health problems, increased stress, and inner turmoil.

However, embracing all of your emotions—learning how to interpret them and then taking action—will allow you to have a life that is in alignment with who you are, decrease your stress, and allow you to live life with intentional joy. Emotions are the brain's way of checking in with you and notifying you that something good or bad is happening. Your brain is giving you feedback about people or events you are experiencing, but you have to learn to interpret the messages.

The first step to interpreting your emotions is cultivating emotional awareness. Emotional awareness includes being able to identify the primary, secondary, or tertiary emotions you are feeling (as identified in the previous section). In addition to understanding your emotion, being aware of your emotional triggers and physiological responses will help you map out patterns and scenarios that give you clarity on what you're feeling. This means you must be in tune with your body. Ask yourself, "How does your body respond to anger, sadness, fear, shame, joy, or surprise?"

Let's use anger as an example. How does your body respond?

Does it feel like a flood of rage internally? Does it feel like heat rising up the back of your neck? In the brain, the amygdala (the part of the brain that deals with emotion) is buzzing with activity. The time it takes to initiate an emotional trigger event and the amygdala's response can be just a quarter of a second. That's why being familiar with your physiological responses before they happen will allow you to be more aware when they are happening in the moment. To illustrate how to interpret your emotions, we're going to take a closer look at two main emotions: sadness and fear.

Sadness

Sadness happens as a result of grief, loss, failure, or some type of disadvantage. We can experience this emotion from something simple, such as losing our favorite shirt or from the passing of a loved one. It's an uncomfortable emotion, and we're sometimes taught as young kids to "cheer up and stop crying" whenever we have been sad. This gives the impression to a child that this emotion should not be explored or experienced but brushed off quickly. However, I believe there are lessons to be learned from sadness if we take the time to interpret the feedback it is providing.

Essentially, sadness is alerting us to loss. If we take time to honor the emotion by understanding what we have lost, it serves a purpose in our lives and allows us to have a better understanding of what we value. Sadness will cause you to take inventory of your life and determine what's important to you. Lean into the emotion and ask yourself questions about what part of the loss did you value.

What characteristics of your friend made you sad? What parts of the relationship are you going to miss? What's lacking for you in this moment? Is it support, acknowledgment, validation, or something else? Use sadness as a tool to re-examine your emotions and get clarity on what you are feeling and why.

Fear

Fear is a distressing emotion that arises from the anticipation of a threat, danger, or pain. Fear can be mild or temporary, but it can also be paralyzing. That could range from a fear of public speaking, worried that you may be publicly rejected, the fear of a relationship breakup, or being unlovable and alone. Fear triggers the flight in our fight-or-flight response, and its purpose is to keep us safe from immediate danger.

The important thing to recognize here is that fear directs us to pay attention to a perceived threat. But on the high end of the spectrum, fear may be alerting us to dangers that are not, in fact, dangers but rather challenges. Fear could occur from doing something that you've never done before or an area of expertise that stretches your capacity beyond the level you are comfortable with doing.

When fear arises, ask yourself: What are you trying to protect me from? Is it really as dangerous as it seems? What is this deeper emotion that the fear is actually based on? Am I afraid of the process or the result? When was the last time I felt this fear? Will I be able to handle this situation differently than the last time I felt this specific fear? Understanding your emotions can help you de- escalate your fear and put that feeling of uncertainty in perspective.

POINTS TO PONDER

This clarity and control will not happen overnight, but being in tune with your emotions and your body will have long-term positive effects. Once you're able to determine your emotional triggers, physiological responses, and your primary emotions, you can move to the next step of interpreting the meaning of the emotion. Our emotions are feedback to let us know what's working well and what isn't working. Emotions help lead us to goals and find a sense of purpose in ourselves, relationships, and our experiences in life. The second half of this book is dedicated to explaining the process of how I learned to apply these principles to interpret my emotions and shift into emotional maturity.

PART TWO:
HOW I REALLY LIVED

CHAPTER 6

SHAME—THE TRIGGER OF ALL MY BUTTONS

I am the first child of my parents and the first grandchild of my family. With that being said, my extended family was extremely excited about my birth. My family made huge investments in me, both financially and in my education. My aunts and uncles pitched in to take care of me, my grandparents drove me back and forth from school, and my mom worked multiple jobs to keep me in private school and allow me to participate in extracurricular activities. They made sure I wanted for nothing and I lacked nothing. So I grew up not wanting to let any of them down.

I always wanted to make sure I pleased them. I wanted to make sure everybody was happy with me and that I received their approval. I wanted to be the straight-A student. I wanted to be the one to make them smile and to know that their investment wasn't wasted. That motivation led to me becoming extremely competitive at times because I didn't like to fail or lose. Since I felt my self-worth was connected to their approval, I didn't like taking second place in any area.

Now, all grown-up, adult Sherese realizes that they just loved me because I was alive. It took some time for me to figure this out. At a very young age, and not at the fault of my family or my parents, I developed a great sensitivity to failure and, more specifically, to shame. I felt like I was the golden child that got everybody's approval and I needed to be an example not only for my siblings but for my cousins. Then, as life always does, it caught up to me.

At twenty-seven years old, I found myself in a marriage that wasn't working. I read all the books, and we even did multiple rounds of counseling. But it didn't work for us emotionally, spiritually, or financially, and I ended up filing for divorce. Now, let me give you a little bit of background about this. I grew up in a Christian home and divorce was not tolerated. Sure, it happened, but by no means was it accepted, except in severe circumstances, meaning in situations of abuse or one spouse cheating on the other.

When it came time for me to file for divorce, not only was I grappling with the decision itself and the failure of our marriage but there also was an overwhelming amount of shame that shook my soul. I had never experienced that depth of shame. I'm talking about the kind of shame that shattered my identity, that destroyed my "good girl" image, broke the golden child halo that I once had, and brought me to my knees. Why? Because I had failed, and I had failed big. I had failed in my marriage. I had failed as a woman. I had failed as a daughter. I had failed and missed my ex-husband's expectations, my own expectations, and my family's expectations.

Through this entire experience, I also became a woman that I was deeply ashamed of becoming. Why? Because I had cheated. Not only was I the one who cheated but I also was the one who filed for divorce. So we're talking about buckets and buckets and buckets of shame. And when I shared some of this information with family and friends in confidence, it didn't actually help because it came up a lot in conversation.

I was told my actions were reckless and childish, and I was called a whore and shunned because I wasn't living up to expectations. This rejection drove me deeper into sadness and left me wallowing in shame. It got to the point that I allowed it to envelop me and send me into depression. I had to spend a lot of time figuring out how I moved from being a golden child and phenomenal role model to losing the respect of family and friends, to crashing and burning—alone. I had to work through the shame of failure and the need for approval that I had developed from my childhood.

When most of us feel shame, the first thing that comes up is feelings of real intense discomfort, inadequacy, guilt, and unworthiness. I wanted to hide, isolate myself, and remove myself from family, my community, and my church. I wanted to separate from everyone and everything that I had been attached to in the prior season. I was consumed with the thought that I was no longer worthy to be called any of the great names or accolades or titles that people have been giving me all my life. Because I was no longer worthy of these things, I wanted to withdraw because I had turned into someone that I didn't even know was there. I didn't even know she existed and wasn't aware of what I was capable of manifesting.

Even more importantly, I felt a lot of anger. I felt a lot of anger toward all the people that I had been there for in times past. I was there when they needed compassion, love, and support, but they were no longer there for me. I covered them in their own shameful moments and upheld them, but they weren't there for me while I was experiencing shame and sadness. I was angry at myself. I was angry at the woman that I had become. I was angry that I had failed in my marriage.

Before it gets too dark in here, I can now say that I appreciate that I went through this experience. It made me who I am today. Every story I'm going to share in this book was an instrument that crafted me into the strong woman that I am today. Had I not experienced these challenges and situations, I wouldn't be able to help other women. I wouldn't be able to help you come out of feeling shame over different areas in your life that you're ashamed to admit you created and you don't want to tell anyone.

IMPACT OF SHAME

Shame will have you believe that it's better that no one knows, to continue walking through life harboring ill will toward yourself, hiding, and disqualifying what you have to offer. You believe if people really knew who you were, and if people really knew what you did, they wouldn't love you or like you. This isn't true. I'm encouraging you to take the lid off your shame and to share whatever has hurt you the most, even if you were the one who caused it. Your most deeply held secrets can hold the greatest amount of shame and actually prevent you from experiencing the life you deserve.

Those unprocessed moments of shame led to a very harsh, self-critical dialogue within. I went from experiencing shame from my divorce to applying the idea that I was fundamentally flawed. I felt it in every single thing that I did, whether that was how I showed up at work, in friendships, or in my relationships with my family. It dictated what I thought I was capable of doing because I don't feel worthy anymore. I felt like something was wrong with me. That's what I heard myself thinking, *I am fundamentally flawed as a woman, and therefore, I'm disqualified.* I'm disqualified to teach, to lead, or to mentor, no matter how much time I took to heal and repair myself.

Over time, I developed this highly self-critical perfectionist inner dialogue. I overcompensated because I didn't want to experience that level of shame ever again. I became highly critical of every word, every action, and every decision that I made because I wanted to stay in the safe zone. Years later, I was still turning down big opportunities and positions because of shame. I was playing small because of shame. I was hiding my capabilities and my gifts. The unrealistic internal guide led me to an obsessive degree of perfection. I wanted to prove myself as I was defending myself.

The overall long-term effects of shame can also manifest as isolation. I isolated myself from my friends, my church, and even at work. The only people that really talked to me in those moments were the persistent ones, like my mom and one of my very good friends, that stayed on me. They didn't let me hide. They didn't let me run. They didn't let me tap out on life. I'm so grateful to my mom for sticking with me in my darkest moments because I would not be here today if it wasn't for her. Her love is one of the ways that helped me process my shameful experiences. When I decided it was time to let go of the shame, the first thing I started to do was look for help.

HOW TO PROCESS SHAME

Therapy

I started seeing a therapist because my shame was too deep, too wide, and too complicated for me to handle alone. I wasn't a professional in this area, but I knew I needed to get myself out of this hole. So I enlisted the help of someone else. My shame was overwhelming to the point that it was affecting my appetite and desire for life and leading to depression. If you feel like you're in that place where any emotions are overwhelming for you, seek help. You need a professional to help you understand your emotions and that can be your guide on your journey. My therapist was able to give me a roadmap from shame to compassion and then to self-acceptance.

I also did my own research and my own work as I went through therapy, so I read a lot of books on shame. Dr. Brenè Brown has done a lot of work on dealing with shame, and I recommend you check out some of her research and books. She has helped me process so much internally, even after I finished therapy. It's a process and journey that is continuous. Dr. Brown speaks a lot about shame resilience and how to develop it so that you can lead a fuller and developed life.

Understanding your triggers

I also had to understand my shame triggers, whether that was in a relationship, experiences at work, or family interactions. I had to get clear on what provoked me and develop a plan to intercept my normal response to shame and rewire my thoughts around the interaction. For example, I have a friend that has shame around her money issues. She subscribes to the idea that her friends and family think she's broke and needy and always in need of help.

Unfortunately, that means any conversations around money that involve her paying for something trigger shame. She becomes easily offended, assumes the worst, and projects her fears on others, forcing her to become defensive.

Understanding your physiological response to shame

After identifying my triggers, I also identified my body's physiological response to shame. This alerts me when I start feeling shame that I need to intercept my automatic response. I know that my body is going into fight-or-flight mode as my body gives me natural cues for me to check in with myself. When I start feeling shame, my physical reaction is to draw myself inward, which means, I'll curl my shoulders and kind of lower my head a bit. I want to turn inward so my body will begin to turn inward. My heart rate will rise, my hands will start to feel clammy, and my face gets flushed from the reaction to shame. When I start to feel those things, and I'm in tune with my body, I can intercept my automatic reaction to snap back with a snarky comment or make a harsh judgment of myself.

These physical cues allow me to check in with myself and think, Hey, Sherese, think this through—you're having a shameful moment. This gives me a chance to switch my path. I know I'm having a shame experience and now I have a moment to pause and make a different choice.

Practicing compassion

The fourth thing that makes a big impact when processing shame is practicing compassion. This is highlighted in Dr. Brenè Brown's quote, "If you put shame in a petri dish, it needs three things to grow exponentially: secrecy, silence and judgment. If you put shame in a petri dish and douse it with empathy, it cannot survive." I had to learn to develop greater inner compassion for my mistakes and my errors.

I would remind myself that when I feel moments of shame, I need to give myself grace. I don't have to be perfect. I don't have to have all the answers. I don't have to present a flawless idea or flawless conversation to share my heart. It's OK to be wrong, to have errors, or make mistakes. I have to verbally repeat that to myself, out loud: "I give myself grace. I give myself grace." Because my instinct is to be harshly self-critical, I acknowledge I made a mistake and repeat those words before my inner critic has a chance to chime in. I also take time to breathe through it. I take about four or five deep breaths, calm my body down, and then move forward.

Then I look for someone to talk to about what happened.

I find someone to share it with because, as Dr. Brown said, shame needs secrecy, silence, and judgment to grow. Find someone to talk to about what is going on in your life. Can you call someone? Can you text someone? Can you tell them what's going on and how you're feeling and talk your way through it with them? Let them know exactly what happened.

For example, at work, I received an email from a team that reviews our reports in fine grammatical detail. They had a lot of comments about my report that I didn't like, and I was annoyed. So I decided to forward the email to my manager and make a sarcastic comment about the team's review of my report. But I accidentally sent the email directly back to the team that reviewed my work, and I panicked. I tried to retrieve the email as quickly as possible as I felt my body go through the full shame experience. I started sweating, my heart was racing, and my senses sharpened because I had to figure out, in five minutes, how to recover this email before they opened it. I was successful in retrieving the email, thank goodness, but the first thing I did was find someone I could talk to about it to prevent the shame from growing. I told my manager.

I shared how I almost made one of the biggest mistakes of my career by talking trash about someone else and sending it directly to them. We both laughed about it, and he showed empathy in that moment and shared how he actually had done the same thing but was unable to delete the email. I felt better about it and let the moment pass rather than continue to beat myself up about it.

So who is that person for you? Who is someone that you can talk to that can walk you through your shameful moments and share with them exactly how you feel what's going on? Give yourself grace, but allow them to give you a moment of empathy as well.

Most likely, they've had a similar experience and it will help you see why it's OK to let go of the shame behind it. This is the easiest way to reap the benefits of the presence of shame.

As I worked through my shame and moved away from the feeling of being fundamentally flawed, I was actually able to accomplish some great things. One big thing was understanding what I needed in my relationships and realizing what I wasn't getting and why. I was able to articulate exactly what I needed in a relationship moving forward. The shame moved me to make some positive changes in my behavior. I would no longer allow myself to live in disharmony with my values or my core beliefs. Know that once you process the shame, you'll be able to uncover some gems from that experience and understand who you are and what you stand for.

POINTS TO PONDER

Understand that unhealthy shame attacks who you are fundamentally and makes you believe that you made a mistake, therefore, you are a mistake. This unhealthy pattern can lead you to withdraw and isolate yourself, force you to focus on accomplishing impossible levels of perfection, and become a harsh self-critic. This can lead you to play small in your life to avoid making mistakes, avoid being vulnerable, and fearing their criticism.

Here's a quick guide on how to process shame:

- Seek professional help when needed.
- Identify your triggers of shame.
- Understand your body's physiological response.
- Give yourself grace in the moment.
- Practice self-acceptance.
- Share your experience with someone close to you.

CHAPTER 7

ANGER–DETONATE IN CASE OF THREAT

When I was a child, my family moved around a lot, and by the time I got to the fifth grade, I was in my fourth new school. I was always the new girl. Being the new girl at school has its challenges, but since three of those four schools were private schools that lacked diversity, I was always the new Black girl in school. More often than not, I was probably the only Black girl in class. I experienced my very first encounter with racism in the first grade.

This young boy was verbally attacking me, upset that I had gotten in line before him and had the chance to be the leader for our line. He made fun of my hair and called me the N-word. I remember feeling so humiliated because, as kids do, everyone laughed at me. I was so hurt and stunned. I didn't know what to say or what to do. I felt my anger begin to rise, and although I wanted to cry, I held back the tears until we made it outside to recess, then I ran to the bathroom to release my tears in private. From that point on, I knew that I would never let anyone else make me feel that way again. The next time someone tried to insult me, they were met with some pretty sharp words and, depending on how angry I was feeling, a swing or two.

And thus began my love affair with anger. I grew up in a household where anger was frequently expressed and was used to control people to get them to do what you wanted, and now I found better ways to use it outside of the home. It gave me a false sense of empowerment. When I arrived as the new Black girl at school, as we continued to move around a lot, I got to work establishing that power. I wasn't one you should mess with because I had a bad temper. I would figure out who was the bully and use my anger and foul mouth to intimidate them. Once I threatened a bully or fought a bully, everyone either wanted to be my friend or was, at the very least, cool with me.

IMPACT OF ANGER

Unfortunately, as I grew out of childhood and school became less threatening, I didn't actually let go of my temper. I continued to use anger as a defense mechanism, specifically, demonstrating to people around me that I had a short temper for anyone or anything that got in my way. Anger became my armor.

The primal emotion of anger is one of the most powerful defense mechanisms you can have. I used that anger to project any personal responsibility I felt for my feelings onto other people. I didn't want to blame myself for feeling hurt and scared of whatever infuriated me or to feel helpless, guilty, or ashamed. I treated family, significant others, friends, and anyone else with the same anger.

What I learned is that anger often limited my emotional growth. I didn't have that many ways to cope with anything that hurt me. My response was first and foremost, always anger. And that, unfortunately, created a lot of stress and anxiety for me, even if I wasn't always aware of it.

You see, I was experiencing a physiological response. While the stress of anger was heightened, I was actually experiencing a reduction in my psychological stress because my body began to secrete adrenaline and that biochemical shift made me actually feel stronger in the moment. It was a way to make me feel temporarily empowered, and I felt like I was in control.

But the overall increase in physiological stress took its toll on my body. Carrying around so much firecracker anger, having a short temper, and pent-up negative energy led me to have double ear infections, walking pneumonia, and migraines. I was a frequent visitor at the doctor's office. It also blocked me from being able to have valuable friendships because I often targeted those around me with my anger whenever I felt hurt, frustrated, or infuriated.

HOW TO PROCESS ANGER

Anger is a feeling of strong dislike or displeasure that is characterized by belligerence as a result of feeling wronged. The reaction can be triggered in conflict, embarrassment, injustice, betrayal, or neglect. As a defense mechanism, it is meant to protect us from danger, as fear does, and it lets us know that one of our boundaries has been violated. Despite its reputation, anger isn't necessarily a bad emotion. It's how we react to the emotion that causes the problems. This is the first part of our fight-or-flight response to danger.

So if I'm angry because I feel that I lacked control or because I've been wronged, I have to ask myself some questions around the anger to help me interpret its presence and take the correct action. Lucky for me, as I was processing my emotions while going through my divorce, I began to question my entire identity. I looked at the areas in which I thought I was weak and places in which I had fallen short. Through my process of self-discovery, I realized I actually didn't like being an angry person.

GETTING TO THE SOURCE OF ANGER

I was tired of feeling a need to protect myself all the time. I decided that if I was going to rebuild myself and let go of the shame, then I had to also let go of the anger so my heart could be healed. I could not be free any other way. I guess you could say that was the gift of my entire meltdown. I got to the source of my anger and discovered I was carrying a high amount of unrectified anger from the past. For me, my anger stemmed from feeling helpless at school, feeling embarrassed or humiliated, or not feeling heard at home. But then I realized I'm not that little girl anymore. I'm not in school, and I don't have to feel like I'm not safe at home. I don't need to fight anymore.

I realized the core hurts and anxieties that I was feeling, such as fear, sadness, helplessness, and humiliation, were at the source of my anger in the first place. I understood that anger helped me conveniently mask those much more disturbing emotions. Until I could identify and work through those emotions that triggered me to become upset and short tempered, I would return to my anger armor again and again. My ego defense reactions were habitual at this point, and my anger was the safeguard for my fragile feelings.

UNDERSTANDING THE PHYSIOLOGICAL RESPONSE

Anger can manifest in my body by a tightening of my major muscle groups, including clenching my jaw and my fists, furrowing my brow, and having a faster heartbeat. I started paying attention to my physiological symptoms of anger, which cued me to slow down. It also helped me become aware of what was triggering me and causing a nasty anger response.

When I first started practicing this technique, I wasn't a pro at managing my anger. I remember getting into a very heated discussion with my dad where we went back and forth for at least a good seven minutes. Then in the heat of this argument, I thought, *Sherese, you're angry and you're responding the old way and not telling him exactly what you're feeling.* So, while he was speaking, I took a moment to pause rather than gear up for my next round of rebuttals. I asked myself why I was really angry and what I really wanted to say.

When he finished speaking, I told my dad how much I respected his words and held him in such high esteem, so when he spoke, his words cut me deeply and made me feel like he didn't love me. That changed the entire conversation. We cut through the back-and-forth rebuttals and got to what I was really feeling. We didn't solve our problems immediately, but it changed the tone. It changed the direction of the conversation, allowing us to both be vulnerable and let down our guard and address the real issues.

POINTS TO PONDER

Anger is a feeling of strong dislike or displeasure that is characterized by belligerence as a result of feeling wrong. It is one of our most powerful defense mechanisms when we feel helpless or when someone has violated our boundaries. The first step to getting to our source of anger is to understand the core emotion. Ask yourself some questions to figure out the source of your anger:

- Are you afraid?
- Are you sad?
- Do you feel helpless?
- Are you feeling humiliated?

Work through these emotions and understand why you feel the way you do. You want to make sure that you're checking into your physiological symptoms of anger. Then you can tap into your awareness and cue yourself to slow down and articulate what you're feeling and determine why something triggered you. This will help you choose a better response.

CHAPTER 8

UNFORGIVENESS— YOU CAN'T CHANGE HOW I FEEL

As I mentioned earlier, I was estranged for six years from the side of my family that had raised me. I hadn't seen or been allowed to speak to my mom, my dad, or younger siblings in California, or my grandparents and extended family in Chicago. Unfortunately, this situation occurred because my dad had started using drugs and our home environment was very unsafe. I asked my mom if I could live with my grandparents until my dad recovered, and she reluctantly agreed. It was all worked out that my grandparents would enroll me in a school near them and take care of me while my parents worked things out. In the meantime, my mom let me visit my biological father and stepmother in the summer and on various weekends.

While my father and stepmother seemingly agreed and supported my decision to live with my grandparents, what I didn't know (nor did my family) is that they were planning to get full custody of me, ignoring the agreement set between my mom, my grandparents, and myself because they felt they knew what was best for me.

One night, my father and stepmother showed up at my grandparents' house with the police to get custody of me. Unannounced. Without preparation. Completely by surprise. Being ripped from the home of my loved ones was absolutely devastating.

Not only did I have to leave my home in California but I also was separated from my grandparents, who provided me with true comfort and love. This whole incident turned into an all-out family war.

I wasn't allowed to see or communicate with any of my family on my mom's side, and it was devastating because that was the only family I really knew. Over time, my biological father and stepmother led me to believe that my mom and the family were upset with me for telling about my stepdad's drug problem, and I was led to believe they didn't want me anymore. To my young mind, it made sense. Why else would my family not call me for my birthday or try to see me for Christmas? I believed that I had ruined everything and was no longer wanted. When my mom gave birth to my little sister, I believed they did it to replace me. I was a hot mess.

I didn't feel wanted and loved by the family that raised me, and by the time I got to high school, I was outright rebelling at home. I wanted to go home but didn't think I would be welcomed, but I also didn't feel at home with my father and stepmother. They put me in private school and let me participate in extracurricular activities, but nothing they tried could address the wound that I felt. I was hurt and I was angry. I was angry with my dad for using drugs and making our home in California unsafe. I blamed him for the upheaval in our family's life and the separation anxiety and depression I felt. But I was also angry with my father and stepmother for lying to me. They had agreed that living with my grandparents would be good but secretly planned to get custody of me without telling any of us. I felt like, at best, it was a failed attempt to show love.

Enter anger, sadness, resentment, and, my good friend, unforgiveness. Unforgiveness is being hurt by the words or actions of another and holding feelings of resentment or vengeance toward them, leading to rumination. When something bad happens, for example, we are in a verbal fight or get laid off, it is easy for our busy minds to go over it again and again. This is how we ruminate and dwell on the situation. This type of thinking causes negative emotions and causes us to get stuck in a rut of deep questions, which can lead to feeling overwhelmed and defeated. In our desire to think it through, we end up digging up negative thoughts from other incidents and link them to what happened, creating a downward spiral of negative thinking. What we ruminate on not only affects our feelings about the offender but also affects our emotions and makes it even more difficult for us to forgive. In addition, unforgiveness is considered a stress response and has an impact not only on our mind but also our health in the long run.

IMPACT OF UNFORGIVENESS

At the age of twelve, I found myself standing deep in unforgiveness and wading into the territory of hate and bitterness. I regularly dwelled in this deep sadness, anger, and resentment which led to increased anxiety, depression, and a decreased immune response. So much so, without any prior family history, I had a severe asthma attack at the age of sixteen. It was a hot summer day in Chicago, and I was experiencing a migraine, so I took some Advil and decided to lay down, but to my surprise, I started to wheeze. I had never had asthma before and wasn't really sure what was going on.

My stepmother, who has asthma, asked me to do a couple of breathing exercises and take her asthma inhaler and lie down. But the wheezing didn't stop, and it felt like I was gasping to breathe. Before I knew it, I started panicking and hyperventilating—on top of having an asthma attack—because I thought I was going to die. It got so bad that my parents ended up calling an ambulance, and I was rushed to the ER. They gave me all kinds of medicine to help my lungs open up, but nothing seemed to be working.

The asthma attack was so bad that I could no longer speak, and my body felt like it had run three marathons and my heart was pumping so hard I felt like I was going to go into cardiac arrest. I actually remember saying to God in my thoughts, *Thank you for a good life. If I die, please let my mom and family be comforted knowing that I loved them.*

As doctors and nurses were scrambling around me, trying to administer treatment and figuring out what to do next, I thought about whether I was ready to leave Earth and give up this life. In my sixteen-year-old mind, I thought I had a good run at things and now was as good a time as any to leave, but then, I thought about my family and how much I missed them. So I said a simple prayer in my head that went like this, *Dear God, I'd really like to see my family again before I die; please don't let me die without seeing their faces one last time.* Shortly after that prayer, my lungs miraculously and slowly started opening up again, and although I couldn't speak, I knew that God heard me as I let the tears roll down my face.

HOW TO PROCESS FORGIVENESS

I was grateful for that recovery, but I didn't realize at that point that my unforgiveness was the reason my health was being impacted. The ER and urgent care asthma visits started to become a regular occurrence and no one could figure out what was triggering it. It wasn't until I got older and started talking to my aunt who had worked on her deep unforgiveness issues that I even realized the two were related. That insight began my journey to healing and forgiveness. I begin to understand that forgiveness was not about condoning the offender's behavior but choosing to accept what happened as it happened rather than being angry with them about how I should've been treated.

Decisional forgiveness

This may sound selfish, but it will drive home the point. I started my journey into forgiveness because I was so tired of being sick. I knew the only way for me to feel better was to start letting go of some of the crap I was carrying around. So the first thing I did was take it to God. I personally had no interest in forgiving any of them. I felt they all wanted me to be angry with them until I died, and I had no intention of letting them change my mind. If it wasn't for God's help in healing my heart from the painful issues, I wouldn't have made it this far. My first step was decisional forgiveness of my offenders: deciding to forgive without the intention of retaliation.

Emotional forgiveness

The second step, emotional forgiveness, was releasing the anger, bitterness, and hate I had toward my offenders. I didn't really have a guide for how to do this, so I went with what felt right for me. I decided to take an afternoon walk and work through every single painful issue that caused me to hold a grudge in my heart. I let the painful experiences arise with the intention of releasing the pain, not ruminating on the past. I allowed myself to replay the events and feel any pain that I had been suppressing or hiding. I allowed it to come all the way out. I think the first time I did it, I had been crying and releasing for four hours straight. I gave God everything: my anger, my hurt, my disappointment, my hate, my rage—every single part of it that took up space in my heart. When I got up from the floor, my heart felt lighter and I felt freer. Everything wasn't OK at that point, but I had started my path to forgiveness, and I had a clear process to healing ahead.

Speak up

My third step meant reaching out to my offenders. I decided to move back to California when I was nineteen, but before I made that decision, I knew I had to talk to my dad about the traumatic events I had last experienced with him. It was so painful for both of us, and I cried as I shared the stories and the emotions that it brought up. My dad, in tears, apologized for what he had done and admitted that he was wrong. We agreed on the boundaries that I needed, he affirmed me as his daughter, and we had a beautiful moment of reconciliation. Over time, I was able to see that this reconciliation brought an even greater level of increased health.

Some years later I reached out to my biological father to have a reconciliation moment with him and discuss the traumatic events that I had experienced. The conversation went quite differently.

There was an I'm-sorry-you-felt-that-way apology but no admittance of wrongdoing and not the kind of closure I thought I needed. It was in that lesson that I finally realized that I didn't need to hear *I'm sorry* for me to forgive anyone.

Forgiveness is always for me, first and foremost, and for the offender second (if they even desire it). I received the benefit of letting it go even if my father didn't understand where I was coming from. I chose to accept his response as it was. That's when I realized that only I had control over the forgiveness. I didn't really need him to admit it or say he was sorry. I was at peace with my father and at peace with my experience.

I know that reaching out to your offender may not be an option for everyone, and in some cases, I chose not to reach out and instead wrote a letter explaining how I was offended and why I was angry. I then wrote a letter to myself from my offender (putting myself in their shoes). It was a healing experience. I shredded the letters once I was done.

POINTS TO PONDER

Unforgiveness is being hurt by the words or actions of another and holding feelings of resentment or vengeance toward them. This often causes rumination. As a result, your body develops a stress response to unforgiveness and triggers a long-term negative impact on your health. Some ways to work through unforgiveness include releasing your emotional pain to God or starting with decisional forgiveness and then moving to emotional forgiveness.

Don't be afraid to articulate your experience to your offender, and if you're unable to do so, try writing a letter to your offender.

CHAPTER 9

GRIEF—HOW AM I SUPPOSED TO LIVE NOW?

Grief: "Hello, old friend. Mind if I take a seat?"

Me: "Umm, I'm kinda in the middle of something called work. Can you come back another time?"

Grief (scans the room): "Great! I think I'll take a seat right here."
Me: "Ugh, it's gonna be one of those days."

I am well acquainted with grief. From experiencing the loss of a loved one, to my divorce, to being laid off from a job, and from the passing of my beloved pet. I thought that as I got older it would be less painful, but instead, I've just learned better ways to cope. My first experience with grief began when I was taken from my grandparents' home and wasn't allowed to see or talk to my family on my mom's side. Though I didn't understand what was happening to me at the time, I know what it was now. I grieved the loving relationships that no longer were around. I grieved the fun times, the laughter, and the joy. I grieved all of the birthday celebrations and the barbecue cookouts and smiles on their faces. I grieved what once was and what I would be missing.

I carried this grief with me every day, and I didn't understand why. I could be receiving an award at school or hitting a layup in a game and wish that their faces were present in the crowd. Every birthday, every Christmas, and every holiday was a reminder that they were not present. Because we typically associate grief with death, it took me a while to recognize my separation grief and to work through it. Besides death and separation, other significant losses can lead to us experiencing grief:

- losing a job that we worked very hard for
- going through a divorce
- having a miscarriage
- children leaving, moving out of the home, or going away to college
- losing a beloved pet (My pet was named little Mama)
- losing a limb or a bodily function
- receiving or being close to someone who received a scary diagnosis (I experienced grief when my grandfather was diagnosed with dementia. Although he was still alive and present, it felt like we were losing him as he transitioned.)

IMPACT OF GRIEF

Grief from these losses might manifest in the form of anger, denial, sadness, despair, and guilt; but it can be different for every person. Grief can lead to intense periods of sadness and rumination. It's a natural response to the loss of a person or thing that was valuable or loved. I've experienced two specific types of grief.

Anticipatory grief

The first type is anticipatory grief, which occurs before the event happens. You may receive advanced notice of a situation, such as you're going to lose your job or you might have a miscarriage.

These are events that could trigger anticipatory grief. It's helpful to know that we can transition ourselves into grief by just being notified that a loss is coming. This type of grief can work in two ways. First, you can find yourself in a painful and confused state while you grieve someone or something that you haven't lost yet. It can be hard to reconcile the impending loss while still being present, and it may be hard to find closure. While it is grief, it can serve a positive purpose. The anticipatory grief will come as a means to help prepare for the loss that is to come. It gives us time to say "I love you," to be there for support, to experience the last moments, and allow us to treasure and honor what was given to us.

I've also experienced anticipatory grief with the passing of my grandfather. I spent the last four years of his life with him. I moved from California to Chicago to help my grandmother take care of my grandfather. When I first moved, we didn't really know what was wrong with him, but we just knew something was off. We went about setting up medical tests, physicals, and appointments, and finally, after eight months of me being there, we were able to get an accurate diagnosis. He was diagnosed with dementia and Lewy body disease. The diagnosis didn't give us a specific timeline of when he might pass, but we researched and found some information to help us gauge how much time he had left.

Once we were aware of the diagnosis, we began to track his progress and see how it was beginning to change him. Now, my grandfather was the patriarch of our family. He was our Superman. He was the person that you called if you were ever in trouble because he always knew what to do. He was a trailblazer, from being one of the first Black delivery persons at his UPS hub to being the first Black minister on staff at his church to being the first Black person on the board of directors at his church.

My grandfather was a strong man, he was a tenacious man, and we knew him as such. With that being said, we also had to come to terms with the fact he was in his transition season. And so the grieving process began. I watched my grandma grieve as she felt that after sixty years of marriage, she was losing her lover and best friend that she had known since she was eighteen years old. She handled it all with grace.

Traumatic grief

Traumatic grief is more likely to be expressed when we're faced with a violent, sudden, or unexpected loss of a loved one. The complicated part about traumatic grief is that while you're experiencing the grief of the loss, you're also experiencing trauma. So traumatic grief can actually be more painful than anticipatory grief. It's easy to find yourself thinking of or recalling something that reminds you of the loved one, and then the painful memories start to flood you and you re-experience your loved one's death, and it doesn't matter where you are or whom you're with—the wave of pain will come.

Unfortunately, the combination of trauma and grief can actually obscure the way to healing and processing your grief because you're trying to work on two things at the same time. For instance, if you had a poor interaction with a loved one right before they passed suddenly without warning, it can be very traumatic, from the way they passed to analyzing your last interactions with them. So instead of being able to focus on releasing the grief of your loss, you may focus on your feelings of deep shame and regret over your last interaction. The shame spiral can take you to emotionally dark spaces and depression that may require therapy for you to begin healing.

As in my case, it also led to an unhealthy bit of hoarding. I tried to hold on to the memories of my loved one through keeping objects or things that didn't even work anymore, were broken, torn, or worn out and probably should have been thrown away. I was afraid that if I threw away those items and the intrinsic value that they gave me, I might forget my loved one, which would add to my grief.

HOW TO PROCESS GRIEF

Belonging and togetherness are part of the human experience.

But the grief process is our natural response to a broken attachment bond. Our job, when we're processing grief, is learning how to cope now that we no longer have this bond.

Give yourself a sacred pause

The first thing I learned when processing grief is to give yourself a sacred time to pause. Don't judge yourself and try to get over it quickly. I've talked to people who have lost their parents, and though it's only been two days, they're already down on themselves, upset that they aren't cleaning the house, cooking, and taking care of their family as they should be. Because grief doesn't have a timeframe, no one can tell you when you "should be back to normal." There's no expiration date on how long you should process your grief and what activities you can and cannot do while you're grieving. Those things are irrelevant. Give yourself the time. When I say give yourself the time, let it be intentional.

I had a family friend pass away. I found out the night before, and I tried to start work the next day, but I found myself sitting at my keyboard with tears running down my face. I couldn't complete any sentences. I felt discombobulated, and I was in a mental fog. I couldn't focus or function. Yet, instead of processing my grief, I beat myself up for allowing it to bother me so much because I had a deadline to meet. I wanted to finish my report and then take time off to grieve, but my heart didn't care about my deadlines. I had to realize and surrender to the fact that I was not OK. I decided that I needed to allow myself a sacred pause, so I took the rest of the day off. I also took the next day off to allow myself proper time to grieve.

Don't try to force yourself to do something that you're not ready to do. You have experienced a loss, a bond that has been broken, and you need time to grieve and to process it in a healthful way. If that means skipping a birthday party, turning down invitations to happy hour, or distracting yourself by going to a movie, then it's OK. You know that you need this space so you can process it healthily. In the long run, you'll be able to ease yourself back into your everyday routine.

Honor what was

I learned to honor what was. When a person that I loved deeply passed away, I took all of his writings, text messages, emails, letters, and cards, and I put them all in one place so I could have them as a remembrance of him and a remembrance of our relationship. It wasn't easy to do, but it was an outlet for me. Whenever I miss him, I open the box and read his words. It was a form of comfort and encouragement for me.

Double Down On Self-care

Be gentle with yourself. In times of turmoil, loss, and grief, you have to double down on self-care. That means paying attention to what you're eating. It's really easy for us to slip into unhealthy eating habits, so we'll eat our favorite comfort foods. But how we eat and what we eat can have a huge impact on our emotional and physical well-being. People respond differently and some may overeat or not have an appetite at all. Dealing with weight loss or weight gain can be an additional complication of prolonged grief.

When you're processing grief, it's natural to have lower levels of energy and motivation. Despite this, you need to implement some level of exercise and physical activity. As soon as you start to feel some level of your energy restored, take that short daily walk around the block. Physical activity is one of the best ways to regulate painful emotions.

Sleep is also extremely important in this time. It can become overwhelming when you are getting text messages, social media messages, and visits while you are making arrangements to lay your loved one to rest. You are expending a lot of mental and emotional energy throughout the day and rest is the key to refueling your emotional tank. Poor sleep makes anyone's life harder, whether you are grieving or not. So try to stick to a sleep schedule. It may not be your regular schedule, but sleep and rest need to be a priority.

Connect with What Gives You Meaning

You should also try to connect with what gives you a sense of meaning. When a loved one or friend passes or you experience a job loss, you start to realize what is important in your life. Reconcile the time that you've been spending and determine how you should spend it moving forward. Does this mean increasing time with family and friends? Do you need to pursue your purpose wholeheartedly? If that means removing fear and anxiety and telling your story and writing your book, do it. Maybe you want to volunteer at a children's hospital and become a magician.

Whatever brings meaning and joy, connect with that.

Ask for Support

Lastly, you want to make sure that you ask for support. I have experienced what I call an attack of grief because it basically feels like it comes without warning. I know a lot of people say that grief comes in waves, but for me, the attacks come without warning, and they hit me hard. I can't stop the tears even if I want to, and I have no control over when it happens or how it happens. It just visits me. I had one such attack as I was on my way to work, sitting on the train. Even though I hadn't consciously realized that I was approaching the anniversary of a loved one's tragic death, my eyes started welling up with tears, and I became overwhelmed with grief. I knew I had twenty more minutes before I got off the train, so I told myself to just breathe through it and I would be fine. I swore to hold back the tears because I was afraid of what complete strangers were going to think of me on the train.

I tried to breathe my way through it for twenty minutes, and I made it to work. I sat down at my desk, but I just couldn't do it. I just started weeping and weeping. It got to the point where I couldn't even speak, so I walked around the corner to my friend's desk. I just put my arms out like a child, gesturing for a hug, and I wept. She hugged me and then took me outside so I could get some fresh air and go for a walk. I shared with her some funny stories about my loved one and her support in that moment helped me get through that very hard morning.

It wasn't like it fixed the entire day, but it helped me get through that difficult morning. Otherwise, I probably would have gone home, gotten under the covers, and spent the entire day bawling my eyes out. Ask for support when you need it. The person may not know what to say or what to do, but just having the comfort of someone being there to hug you, hold your hand, and listen can make a huge difference.

POINTS TO PONDER

Grief is different for every person but can come from a variety of losses that could manifest in the form of anger, denial, sadness, despair. It's a natural response to the loss of a person or thing that was valuable or loved by us. Give yourself a sacred pause to process your grief, honor the memories of your loved ones in a tangible way, double down on self-care, connect with what gives you meaning, and ask for support when you need it.

CHAPTER 10

SETTLING—I THINK I'LL STAY AWHILE

I just finished cursing him out . . . and I don't even curse anymore.

I went all the way back to fifth-grade Sherese. I tapped into her anger and my instincts to protect myself. It was a massively overblown fight! We went from him walking out, slamming the bedroom door, and yelling at me to me throwing a gallon of water down the stairs at him. I reacted in a split second. Once I calmed down, I wondered, *Who am I and where did this behavior come from. Why did I think that this was acceptable behavior in a relationship with someone I loved?*

But that moment of introspection didn't last long because he always came back with great apologies, gifts, and a whole lot of . . . well, you know. That's the kind of cycle I was in. I felt it was normal, and this was the best relationship I could have. I couldn't remember when we began treating each other like this, and I didn't even know how we had gotten this bad.

My boyfriend was cute, charming, confident, generous, and an emotional wreck.

We started with some heavy flirting, and we buzzed around each other for quite some time before he made the move. The beginning of our relationship was amazing. It was fun; we enjoyed each other. We were silly together, and we had some intense happy moments in our relationship. I can't remember when our dispositions began to change with each other.

But our relationship started to expose the unhealed parts of ourselves, and he began lashing out. I would try to be this amazing, good girlfriend: cool, forgiving, accommodating, and supportive.

But, after a while, it began to wear on me. The more he would attack, bully, and lash out verbally and emotionally, the more I regressed to my childhood defense mechanisms. Before I knew it, I was doing things that I never imagined doing, like throwing a gallon of water at someone I loved. The gloves were off and we were in a battle to see who could be the most outrageous.

At first, I justified it, saying it was normal and he just loved hard. I settled for what I thought I could get because I didn't think I could find someone that loved me without toxic anger flares. I allowed this to go on for over a year before I figured out that something was wrong. I allowed it to take its toll on me mentally, emotionally, and physically. I finally figured out I needed to let go of the relationship and deal with some deeper anger issues. At some point, we did try to reconcile as we realized we both were acting in very unhealthy ways and needed to address what was going on.

I don't think that we were equipped to handle our own pain, let alone each other's pain. I started to learn more about his family history and understand his childhood, and that's when some things started to make sense. When he was a child, he was physically abused by his parents. His father would sometimes show him intense love, but only after they would have a really big fight. In his mind, in order to receive love or feel love from me, he would purposely pick fights and push me to my limits because the angrier I got meant the more love that I could show him after the fight.

That's why he subconsciously would trigger big fights so he could feel loved afterward. It was the only way he knew how to receive love.

IMPACT FROM SETTLING

It's one thing to know why something is wrong, and it's an entirely different thing to fix. The effort it takes to apply safety measures and boundaries and prevent yourself from hurting someone emotionally, mentally, and physically requires a lot of inner healing and can't be done on willpower alone. Although we tried, I ultimately ended the relationship.

I understood that there were some issues that I needed to work on independently and heal before I got into my next relationship. I also realized, after coming out of a divorce, I didn't really think I would ever find "the one." Out of fear of being alone and thinking that meeting my ideal partner was a myth, I lowered my standards to simply find a good enough guy. But this ultimately cost me my self-respect and was a major blow to my self-confidence. After the breakup, I focused on doing the inner work of healing. The first thing I asked myself was, "Why did I choose this guy?" The answer was daunting.

THE WAYS WE SETTLE

Why do we settle? Usually, it stems from fear or using another to fix your issues.

Childhood wounds

Daddy. Wounds. Are. Real. Unless you are aware of it, we often seek the same dynamic in our romantic relationships that we experienced in our childhood. It comes from an unconscious desire to repair the father (or mother) wound by having a relationship with a person that created similar feelings with you in your childhood.

We gravitate to that type of person because it's familiar, we understand how to deal with them, and simultaneously, we have the chance to possibly heal our childhood wounds.

My dad loved me like crazy, loved our family like crazy. We had intense high moments of joy and celebration of love, but we also had volatile moments that included bursts of anger, harsh criticism, and snap judgments. My boyfriend's behavior mirrored my childhood experience. It wasn't until we were talking and he said something that made me connect the dots. He said, "I think you handle me so well because I remind you of your father." I didn't want to receive that. I didn't want to believe it. But the more I thought about it, I knew he was right. He reminded me of my dad; the good times and the bad times. I knew if I didn't heal this part of my heart, I would continue to attract men who I thought would help me heal my childhood wound.

Dating from A Deficit

We cannot date from a relationship deficit. What do I mean by that? When you finish going through a really bad breakup, whether you were dating someone or coming out of divorce, sometimes we will tell ourselves, "I won't date anyone like that ever again. I'm going to date someone who is not like him at all." I realized that I had created fragments of what I was looking for in a relationship and not the whole picture. Every time I ended a relationship, I fixated on a new fragment. Then I would vigorously search for the new fragment in someone else. Without a complete overview of the person, I would dive in because I found the fragment I was looking for. But in the end, I was chasing just that fragment.

So if your ex was lazy, didn't like vegan food, and was a homebody, you may decide to date someone who is spontaneous, loves adventure, and likes all types of foods. If your ex was someone who was serious, didn't like to laugh or play much, was very focused on his business, or was obsessed with working out all the time, you look for someone who's the complete opposite of that. You're looking for someone to fulfill the deficits that you acquired from your previous relationship.

That is one of the worst mistakes that we can make when we start dating again. Just because my ex wasn't spontaneous doesn't mean I need someone super spontaneous. I may just want someone who likes to explore sometimes. The problem is I used the next person to help me heal from a previous relationship.

Emotionally unavailable

I had a problem attracting emotionally unavailable men. I did this mainly to protect myself. Now, I never told myself any of this consciously, but it was definitely a pattern for a reason. I didn't want to expose who Sherese really was. I didn't want to reveal my innermost secrets, my idiosyncrasies, or anything that made me look bad. I subconsciously plotted to attract someone who was emotionally unavailable, so I could only love and enjoy them to a point. But I knew we would only go so far. Dating emotionally unavailable men would ensure a level of protection for me to help me avoid being vulnerable.

HOW I STOPPED SETTLING

There are a couple of techniques that I used to heal myself. The first thing that I determined was that I had to get clear on my values. Our values are our principles. They are our guide; the virtues of what we deem necessary for a healthy and happy life. My personal values need to be reflected in the person that I am dating if I hope for any long-term compatibility.

This realization caused me to get clear on my non-negotiables.

What did I need in a partner? What values am I unwilling to compromise? I wanted a generous man of faith with integrity, who was an entrepreneur (or aspiring). He needed to have compassion and be family oriented. Those were the type of values that I determined were non-negotiable. When we aren't clear on our non- negotiable values, it's really hard to date someone that will be compatible. In the long run, the relationship is not going to last because you don't agree on what's important.

Purpose vs. Preference

In addition to my values, I had to be clear on my personal purpose. I can't expect my relationship to work if our purposes do not complement each other. More often than not, we get caught up in feeling chemistry and date for preferences. We're looking at the fact that he's attractive, tall, doesn't have any kids—these are preferences. We will date someone that has these preferences in place, but they may not be a good match for our purpose.

If you are someone who desires your own business and your partner does not, your partner may not support you and may think that it's reckless, putting an extra strain on your relationship. Before you get that far, you have to get real clear now. Understand, it doesn't matter how great those preferences are; it's not going to work out. Date someone who can handle your purpose. Don't let your preferences be the only light guiding you. Let your purpose and your values guide you to the type of person you should be dating.

The tragedy of dating only for preference further supports why you cannot date from a deficit. You will always change what you need from person to person and may compromise yourself or your standards to make the relationship work. It's going to be really hard for you to find someone who matches your values and complements your purpose if you are only considering your preferences.

Be authentic

I learned that I cannot be all things to all people. What does being authentic mean? I cannot be the girl that bites her tongue so I can come off as cool and nice. I can't keep transforming myself so they can love me or date me or think that I'm worthy of a committed relationship. If you don't like something, speak up. When you are in a relationship, your first impressions are lasting impressions. You show people how to treat you by what you allow and what you refuse to allow to happen.

I spent a significant amount of time trying to explain and justify my value. In the end, I realized he could never recognize my value because we were on a different measurement system. As women, no matter how much we try to convert our scales (become who they want us to be), in the end, we're just being devalued. Be cautious of modifying your behavior when you come out of a relationship and start a new one. Sometimes, because we are in a vulnerable space and we're really just looking for someone to validate that we are worthy of love, we will subconsciously start changing for them.

For example, if you really like cuddling and being close and he doesn't like it as much, don't adjust yourself for him. What you're effectively saying is that physical touch is your primary love language, but you are willing to accept less in your love tank. Why accept less? It will only lead to arguments, tension, and leave you unfulfilled in the relationship. Don't let the need for validation and acceptance change who you are because your alteration will only be temporary. At the end of the day, who you truly are, what you believe, what you value, and what you want in a relationship is going to come out. When it comes out, it will be under all the stress and pressure you placed it under, so it's not going to be pretty.

You're basically giving them your representative, not who you truly are.

Do not ignore the red flags

I was always hoping and looking for the best and I ignored red flags and warning signs to a fault. I would get caught up in how outgoing he was. He's so funny. Oh, he's generous. He's so tall. Those few good preferences would overshadow the other bad things in the relationship and blind me to the red flags. Evaluate each characteristic of your partner, independently, and question if this person never changes, would you marry them as they are today.

Do not fall in love with potential because I'm going to tell you this: you cannot change anybody but yourself. There is no guarantee, with all your prayers, counseling sessions, and couples classes, that your partner will ever change. Trust me. I've been there. You have to accept them exactly where they are. If you can be honest and say that if my partner does not change, I would not marry him, then you know your answer. You may be in love with a version of your partner that does not exist.

Do not expect him to change and don't make any plans to make him change. Accept him as he is, or not at all. If you are plotting on his potential and hoping he will change, you are ignoring red flags. Ideally, you meet someone, start a relationship, plan to build a life together, and encourage and support each other along the way. If you get into the relationship and you're already picking out things that you want him to change and do differently, it will end badly.

Trust me.

Learn how to receive

I'm analytical and usually in a position of authority, so learning how to receive took me a while to learn. I am the giver. I would spend a lot of time pushing things forward, driving things to get done, reaching goals, and I wasn't in a receiving place. It felt weird allowing things to come to me, taking my time to blossom, or receiving gifts. It was hard for me to surrender something so simple, like letting my partner plan where to go on vacation. I didn't know how to surrender to the moment and let my partner lead. My inability to relax and receive led to me overanalyzing my partner's steps and telling him how it should have been done.

The inability to receive came from two places. I had a fear of being indebted to anyone for anything. In times past, it was used as manipulation to coerce me into action, and I resented it. I would get anxiety over owing the giver something in return. I also found it hard to receive because I had a fear of being unworthy. Why would anyone want to do that much for me if I haven't given them that much yet? I struggled with being worthy as my natural state. I had to work through my false beliefs to open up my heart to naturally receive and surrender.

POINTS TO PONDER

Settling for less than what you want or deserve comes from the emotion of fear. We think that meeting our ideal partner is a myth, so we lower our standards to simply find a guy who is just good enough. Make sure that you date someone that matches your values and your purpose, in addition to your preferences. Be authentic in your relationship and don't show up as the partner you think they want. Evaluate all red flags and warning signs independent of your partner's good traits. Learn how to receive and surrender if you are used to being the one who always gives.

CHAPTER 11

STRESS—I'M SUPER WOMAN, AND I DON'T NEED TO REST

This was my second visit to the ER in one week, and they couldn't figure out what was wrong with me. I was having trouble breathing, but upon the second visit, they admitted me to the ER. That visit turned into, "Oh, you have pneumonia," which turned into a longer stay at the hospital, two weeks to be exact, before they were ready to release me. By the third week, I was allowed to go home but given notice to be on bed rest for at least another week before I started moving around again or went back to work. I was so angry and frustrated with my body. Here we go again. I can't catch a break.

I was upset that I had to stop running around because my body shut down on me. My body went haywire on me because I was working full time, forty hours a week, and I was also working a part-time job, ten hours a week. I was volunteering probably another ten hours a week. To top it off, I was also in graduate school, pursuing my Masters in Business Administration (MBA). I had taken on a lot of responsibilities and spread myself thin, mentally and physically. It wasn't until my body shut down completely that

I realized it really wasn't my body's fault, but that I had actually done this to myself.

IMPACT OF STRESS

That's when I really started to dive into understanding my stress and my triggers. Stress is the body's reaction to any kind of demand or threat. It can come from a thought or an event that makes you feel frustrated, nervous, or angry. But not all stress is bad. In short bursts, stress can be useful for survival, like running away when you see a rattlesnake in the grass, or when you need to meet a deadline. But long-term stress? That's when the body goes off track. Stress is triggered by the amygdala, nuclei located deep in the temporal lobes of the brain, which triggers chemicals to be released into your body that helps you get through stressful times. These chemicals impact your cardiovascular system, your digestive system, your blood pressure, and your heart rate.

My body was operating under long-term stress—in constant fight-or-flight mode—and never received the signal that I was no longer under threat. All of the events and circumstances in my life led to an accumulation of stress that created serious health problems. I eventually learned not to repeat those behaviors and habits after that last ER visit. I had to start saying no to some requests and also start saying yes to help. I struggled with receiving help and loved being the constant giver. The imbalance took a toll that I was no longer willing to pay.

SELF-CARE TO THE RESCUE

I realized, in that moment lying in the hospital bed, I couldn't continue to give other people what I haven't learned to give myself. I cannot pour from an empty cup. I had to work on taking care of Sherese. I had to make sure I got adequate sleep, that I was eating well, resting, and spending some time decompressing and restoring. In other words, I needed to practice self-care. But I was convinced, through years of belief, that self-care was not important. Asking for help was not important. I told myself many false beliefs:

- When I receive something, I'm obligated to give something in return.
- I only accept what I feel I deserve to have.
- The giver has the power to take it away, and I don't want to experience loss.
- I was raised to be independent and strong; being needy is weak.
- Asking for help would be too much of a burden on other people.
- It's wrong to ask for what you want, and I don't like being wrong.
- Other people need help more than me. I would be selfish to take it.
- I've been blessed with more, so I have an obligation to give and never take.
- Kindness is not always sincere. Is there an ulterior motive?
- Struggling is honorable. If something was easy, then it wasn't earned.

My beliefs placed very harsh judgments around receiving help and saying no and damaged my ability to really receive love, connection, and support. You see, we often believe that we have to be strong and independent and able to handle everything on our own, and asking for help is a sign of weakness. This idea often comes through our culture, overgeneralized concepts about women, or even our own families.

HOW TO DECREASE STRESS

The first thing I learned is that you have to allow yourself to be vulnerable. Accepting help requires that you have to give up some degree of control. I didn't really like that. I felt that if I wasn't in control, then I ran the risk of being in danger, and accepting help puts me in a weak, vulnerable position. But actually, vulnerability isn't something to be deemed as weak. Being vulnerable requires strength. It requires us to surrender to whatever is being given.

When we surrender, it frees us up from having to lead, navigate, or drive. Instead, we get to enjoy receiving and have an opportunity to explore and appreciate what is given. It was easier for me to use defense mechanisms to protect myself from getting hurt than it was to ask or receive help. The truth is, my defense mechanisms were blocking me from receiving love, and I ultimately ended up hurting my body.

Culturally, deep emphasis is placed on women to give help to others. However, this is a flawed and imbalanced way to develop. Women typically do a lot of the giving in relationships, whether it is raising children and providing their needs or supporting others. If we are giving without receiving, we naturally become imbalanced. It may not show up today, tomorrow, or next year, but eventually, we will feel the effects and have to reconcile the imbalance.

You do yourself a complete disservice to ignore, deny, and block your ability to receive. The human body and spirit are resilient, but we can only endure so much to a certain point before it breaks down. The key is not to force your body into a continuous defensive state. There is a time to battle and a time to rest, and rest itself is a weapon for our defense.

We also don't ask for help because somewhere along the line we believed we were not worthy to receive help. This type of thinking can develop if you received a form of conditional love we received in childhood and early adulthood. The need to feel like you must perform, give something in exchange, or feel worthy to receive handicaps our ability to receive.

Similarly, we don't ask for help because we believe we will be in debt to the person that helps us. But because you are a giver and are constantly releasing love, time, gifts, and attention to others, you automatically put yourself in a position to receive a harvest from what you've sown. Don't allow someone's perverted attempt to abuse the purpose of a gift make you disown your harvest. People who you've never invested in will come to sow and give to you.

That's OK too. What you give is not guaranteed to come back in the form you gave it in, but it still comes back to you. It's a universal principle of giving.

When we're constantly releasing and giving to others but don't allow ourselves to receive, we're choosing to put ourselves on a course for a crash, burnout, or a nervous breakdown. There should be an equal flow of releasing and receiving. If the cycle becomes imbalanced, we lose order and something or someone will begin to suffer for it. It's not a matter of need, or proving yourself, or being abnormally strong. It's a matter of order. And refusing to receive means you are out of order.

The natural order of sowing is to receive, hold, and release. What you do in the hold determines the impact of what you release. What you release will always be greater than what you received. But if you are not receiving anything, how can you multiply nothing and give double? It doesn't make sense. If I asked you what zero times zero was, you'd accurately answer zero. Anything times zero will always be zero and our emotional and physical selves are no different. You cannot get around this principle.

Let's do a breathing exercise. I want you (without inhaling) to try and hold your breath for twenty seconds and then release. Now, unless you have really good lungs (or if you didn't follow directions and inhaled first), you would find that holding your breath without inhaling (receiving air) first creates a slight choking sensation. Your body starts to send a signal that you need air. Now let's try the same exercise: hold your breath for ten seconds (without inhaling); after ten seconds, release a little bit of air; wait five seconds and release a little more air; wait five seconds and release a little more air; then release the air you have left in your lungs. Did you notice that it got harder and harder to release air without an inhalation (receiving air) to start? This is what happens to many mothers when they don't practice self-care. This is what women do when they feel they have to prove they're strong and not weak.

So to decrease your stress, you need to learn to receive. And then to do that, you need to understand your physiological response, embrace the moment, and accept help.

Understanding my physiological response

Receiving is not something that comes naturally to me. It's something that stays in the forefront of my mind when someone asks if they can help me. In the past, I would receive help or gifts and those favors would later be thrown in my face and used as a manipulation or negotiation tactic. I developed a fear response around it to prevent myself from having the painful experiences again.

My body was primed to alert me that when someone offers to help, I could be opening up myself for a repeat painful experience. My shoulders would tense up, my stomach would tighten, and I quickly responded to someone that offered me help with an instant "No, thank you." Pay attention to your body and how it responds. It is going to cue you in that you're starting the process of creating a stress response. That cue can give you the time to breathe and intercept your next move.

Embrace the moment

When I'm not comfortable with receiving something, my instinct is to try to return it immediately. For instance, if someone compliments me on my dress, I compliment them on their hair. If someone says, "I love you," of course the response is to say, "I love you too." But have you ever had someone tell you they love you and you didn't want to say it back, but you felt bad for not reciprocating it? That demonstrates my point exactly. We aren't comfortable with just receiving it in one direction. It makes us feel selfish to not immediately give back.

My new practice is when it's time for me to receive, I realize that it's important for me to just pause and embrace the moment. I don't have to be in a rush to give something back to the other person. I don't have to deflect what they said, as if I can't receive from them and must give it back immediately. Think about it. When someone compliments you and you weren't thinking about complimenting them, but you give them an immediate compliment in return, it kind of comes off as inauthentic.

In regard to love, if someone shows you love by helping you or assisting you in any way, true love keeps no record of wrong. It also does not keep a record of who is winning. There's no score, so there's no need to return the love. This is not a competition; just receive it. It's healthier to wait until it's an appropriate time for you to give, and then you can return the favor of love.

Accepting help

Accepting help takes practice. You can just start saying yes to any responsible person that asks you if you'd like assistance. If you're checking out at Home Depot and they ask if you would like help to your car, say yes. If you're lighting a bonfire at the beach and someone asks you if you need help carrying the wood, then hand them the wood. Look for a moment for you to practice receiving and saying yes. There are so many things that we receive every day. We can practice gratitude for receiving the sunshine and for the rain. Having a moment to just pause, breathe, and appreciate what you are receiving can help shift you from fear and anxiety to being in the flow of abundance and receiving even more.

POINTS TO PONDER

Stress is the body's reaction to any kind of demand or threat. It can come from a thought or an event that makes you feel frustrated, nervous, or angry. Not all stress is bad. You can process and control your stress by deciding that you will allow yourself to be vulnerable and ask for help, understanding your body's physiological response, learning to embrace the moment of receiving help, and practicing accepting help.

CHAPTER 12

ANTI-SELF—I WISH I WAS (FILL IN THE BLANK)

> Personal Journal Entry
> Date: August 18, 2018
> Time 8:18 a.m.

I am Sherese Shy-Holmes. I no longer reject myself, who I am, my authority, or who I am meant to be, and what I am meant to do. I command my whole self to come into alignment and congruence with who I am authentically. I am not afraid of myself. I am not ashamed of my story. I am not distancing myself from who I was and who I am, I embrace all of me. I am gracefully me; I am not afraid of my voice, and I am not ashamed.

Reaching the point where this was my journal entry was a long journey. I have always been highly critical of myself, so add in a dash of perfectionism and a dollop of people pleasing, you've got a real recipe for disaster. I call this a recipe for anti-self. The phrase anti-self, to me, is a nice way of saying that I had some level of self- loathing. I know that sounds extremely harsh, so I want to break that down for you.

I have been one of those people that would say, "Yes, I love myself, I love me. I know my worth and I'm not taking less than what I deserve." But those were just words. If you pull the layers back and you look at my actions, my deeds, how I handled myself, you would see that I didn't necessarily hate my entire life, but I definitely didn't demonstrate in actions that I loved myself. Love is an action verb. I was only saying the words.

Love is not just an emotion. I think we get really confused when we hear the word self-love and think that it's some sort of emotion that demonstrates we love ourselves. Instead, look at your actions. Ask yourself these questions:

- Do you have boundaries?
- Do you rest enough?
- Do you support your creative endeavors?
- Do you put yourself down often?
- Do you give yourself a proper meal with adequate nutrition?
- Do you practice self-care?
- What's your body image like? Do you dislike and speak negatively about parts of your body?

Those are simple questions that we can use to gauge how much we are actively demonstrating love to ourselves. It will help you determine whether it's just talk or if it's actually real to you. The opposite of self-love is anti-self. To better explain it, I want to dive into self-loathing, which I think accurately depicts an understanding of the levels of anti-self behavior. Self-loathing is a fear-based feeling that you are not good enough as you are. It's a harsh inner critic reminding you of your inadequacies. It usually causes us to compare ourselves to others, to put ourselves down, and disown our magnificence. My harsh inner critic has tried to tell me many negative things:

- My life sucks compared to everyone else.
- Why is my life so bad?
- My stomach is too big. Don't wear that. I need to cover it up.

- I don't have the body for that dress.
- I still haven't gotten married yet. Something must be wrong with me.
- I'll always be single.
- I'm probably cursed.

That last one cracks me up, but I genuinely used to believe that all the misfortune in my life resulted from me being cursed. I had no reasonable proof that I was cursed or that curses were even real, but my inner critic told me it was so, and I believed it. I listened to this inner critic berate me and scold me, and I never questioned it. Instead, I battled my inner critic by trying to exhibit the opposite of what I was feeling.

For example, if I wasn't feeling like I was enough, I would cover it up and present myself as strong, confident, and carefree. My defense mechanism was overcompensating. Now don't get me wrong. There's nothing wrong with faking it until you make it, but that will only get you so far. When does it actually become real to you? It becomes real when you're no longer faking it but feeling it, and when you deal with the root of the issue.

IMPACT OF THE ANTI-SELF

After going through my self-discovery process and some years of inner work, I realized my self-loathing came from a negative early life experience. After all, my caretakers could be highly critical of themselves, about their weight, their accomplishments, their lack of money, lack of education, and lack of opportunities. Their verbal discussion of self-judgment taught me how to judge myself. And when someone is talking to themselves that way, the same negative self-talk would be used when they would talk to me. Before I knew it, I had a committee of critics in my parents, aunts, uncles, caretakers, teachers, coaches, and mean friends. They all lived in my head as one internal negative coach.

What's the impact when you have a negative coach that outweighs all of the great and positive things that you're doing and accomplishing in your life? Well, I've shared a couple of examples in the previous chapters, but it definitely has an impact on the kind of friends and partners you choose. Why is this? Because you train the people in your life on how you want to be treated. They will treat you in proportion to how you think of yourself and no less. If you're wondering why you keep attracting poor-quality partners, it has something to do with the way you think about yourself. In addition, we start to use this negative internal coach as a filter.

We believe that how we think of ourselves is exactly how other people view us. It causes us to become skeptical, paranoid, and we start disconnecting from quality relationships. We tell ourselves,

"How could they love me if they know I'm a failure?" Our next move is to reject the love we're receiving, project our internal negative feelings on them, and then sabotage the relationship. In the meantime, we think we have done ourselves a favor by breaking up with them to avoid the future heartache, not realizing that our anti-self thinking was the initial cause.

Most people are very unaware that they are looking at life through this lens. If someone tells me something positive that is the opposite of what I'm used to hearing from my negative internal coach, I believe that something is wrong with them: they may have an ulterior motive, they're lying to me, or they're not being genuine. I'm questioning the investment they're willing to make in me because I am not confident in who I am.

This actually is a reflection of my lack of self-love because I didn't challenge the harsh judgments of a negative internal coach and normalized it since childhood. Roll all of that together, and you have a beautiful girl living in fear and phobia of imagined limitations and filled with self-loathing. I was a girl who was playing small on everything in order to avoid being found an impostor.

HOW TO HEAL FROM THE ANTI-SELF

The first step is identifying the inner critic by thinking about your childhood experiences. Can you recall some of the harsh words that you remember being heard? What were some of the words that were actually said to you that caused you to develop a negative internal coach? I commonly thought, *If I decide to be a dancer and not get a degree in accounting, everybody will be mad at me. If I decide that I don't want to marry this guy, and I still want to be single, everybody's going to say I'm stupid.*

Identify your everybody

I want you to identify your *everybody*. I'm pretty sure that you're not going to be able to come up with more than just three people. Guess what? There is no everybody. By using an absolute word, like everybody, you are exaggerating and using hyperbole, which we explored in the chapter on defense mechanisms. Really, it's only a couple of people that have been in your life and have shaped your ego, your conscious, and subconscious mind. Identify who those people are, remember the words you heard them say, and get to the root of the issue.

One way to identify and track the negative internal coach is to keep a thought journal. You can jot down any negative internal dialogue that you receive throughout the day. Write down any random negative thoughts that you say about yourself, people, events, and anything that happened. In the evening, analyze your thoughts and figure out what patterns are developing. Make no mistake: the negative statements you make about others are also a reflection of your internal negative critic. Are there certain triggers that happen before your negative thoughts?

Challenge the negative internal coach

Once you identify the people and the destructive thoughts and attitudes that they help to internalize, it's time for you to challenge that critical inner voice. How do you challenge that voice? You start with compassion. Self-compassion is being understanding of ourselves when we experience perceived instances of inadequacy, failure, or loss. Think of it as treating yourself the same way you would treat a friend who came to you after failure. Would you respond to them with a demoralizing tone or with empathy? What words would you use to comfort them?

When you respond with compassion to the critic, you're inserting a level of grace and a measure of truth. This will allow you to free your heart and help you remove the negative lens so you can get an accurate picture of what is being said and what is being done.

Letting your negative internal critic run the show is like living in an alternate reality. Imagine you're watching a 3D movie without the 3D glasses. It's going to look highly distorted. You can kind of gauge the images and loosely speculate what's on the screen. But until you put the right glasses on to watch the movie, or use the right lens to view a situation, you won't get a clear picture. Your negative internal coach is giving you a blurred and skewed picture of life and how other people are treating you, and you've got to challenge it.

Give yourself some statements of compassion that will help you challenge those negative thoughts when they arise.

Develop affirmations

Affirmations are a good way to do this. Affirmations are assertive statements that firmly declare a positive belief to challenge and overcome self-sabotage and negative thoughts. But in order for you to challenge those negative thoughts, you have to practice saying affirmations on a consistent basis. Affirmations are not a quick fix but a long-term remedy. You don't just say them when you're hearing your negative internal coach; you need to practice affirmations when you're feeling good. Imagine it as though it were a game of ping-pong. When the negative internal coach pops a negative thought in your direction, you can take your ping-pong paddle and deflect it with your positive affirmation. You have to practice and train your mind to be ready with a response. Use your words to smack that ball back to the other side of the table or across the room.

Set a timer on your phone and remind yourself to say your affirmations throughout your day, or say them in the morning when you get started and in the evening before you go to bed. You'll begin to train your mind to believe the opposite of what your negative internal coach is telling you, which will create a barrier of resistance when the negative thoughts come your way.

POINTS TO PONDER

Self-loathing is counterproductive to your full and productive life.

It can impact how you feel about yourself and your future, and cause you to make inaccurate judgments through the voice of your negative internal coach. The best way to counter the negative internal coach is by creating a thought journal to identify patterns, and then develop affirmations to counter the negative thoughts.

CHAPTER 13

COMPARISON–IT'S THE PICTURES FOR ME

We talk about staying woke all the time, but then we slip into traps like comparison every single day, sometimes multiple times a day. But why? Leon Festinger said, in 1954, that we use comparison as a form of evaluation and we have an internal desire to evaluate our abilities and performance with that of other people.

Unfortunately, if we don't have objective information about our performance, we'll compare ourselves to others. This is how we determine whether we're on track or if we should do something different. Thus, comparison is more or less how we measure our success.

Sadly, we take note of what everyone is doing on social media, and in essence, measure our entire lives against someone else's happy moments. A study conducted by the University of Pennsylvania found a causal link between time spent on social media and loneliness or depression. The more time the students spent on social media, the greater their feelings of loneliness or depression.

Although everyone struggles with comparison, I believe women have a unique struggle when it comes to the issue. There's pressure in the media and in our culture that women should be able to do it all. We are fed the idea that we should be the ideal woman who has a successful career, keeps a beautiful Pinterest-inspired home, is a phenomenal mom, cooks delicious meals that would make Chef Gordon Ramsay jealous, and maintains a beach-ready body. It's. All. Overwhelming.

Let's break down what comparison is so we can stop the cycle.

Comparison is actually composed of shame, scarcity, and fear. Here is what that looks like below:

THE COMPARISON PYRAMID

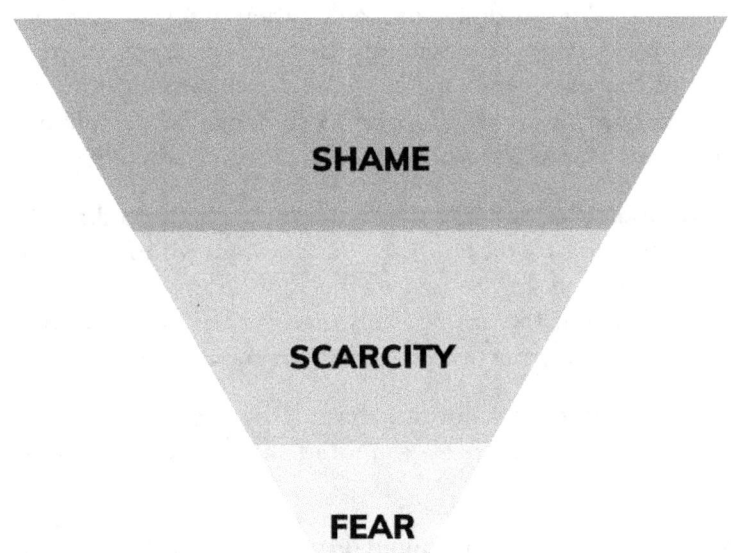

SHAME

When I see a life coach seemingly get 50,000 followers overnight, I can feel ashamed of my low follower count. I see a friend buying a home and feel ashamed I don't have my own house yet. I see washboard abs and think about my bloated stomach, feeling ashamed that I don't take the time to work out to the degree I would need in order to get those abs. I see beautiful photoshoots in exotic locations while I sit at home in my leggings, wondering what amazing new thing I'll notice in the backyard today.

We need to take a step back and realize that most people are only sharing their highlights on social media. We are only seeing what they perceive to be successes. Just because they come across living fuller lives doesn't mean that they have achieved more than us or even feel good about themselves. Are they insecure and post filtered beauty shots to get compliments? Social media is not real life. Along with the false comparison on social media, we also have a false season comparison. I fall into the habit of discounting my personal season by comparing it with someone else's life. I'm ashamed that I'm not doing as well as they are. It makes me think that I'm not working hard enough or that I missed an important element to success. It took me a while to understand that it's pointless to compare my winter season to someone else's summer. Our winter seasons have a purpose too. Let me explain why.

I read an article that said perennial plants have to die in the fall so they have time to expand their root system without focusing on providing nutrients to the rest of the plant. Perennial plants send up fresh growth in the spring. This means that our more dormant seasons, specifically our winter season, is a necessity for growth.

The root system is enlarged during this time, which means in your winter season, you are expanding through your learning and life lessons.

Winter is also a time for an environmental reset. Rest is a mandatory period for Earth and all of life. It's necessary for restorative balance; everything dies to be reborn. While you're comparing yourself to others, take some time to examine where you are at. Are you in your winter season expanding your roots? Is this a season of rest so you can release something new in the coming season? In addition, the strong root system established during the fall and winter season creates a stronger plant. You can focus on developing your foundation and essential areas in your life that need more love, time, and attention from you. All of our seasons in life have a purpose and they should be respected, not despised.

There are new adventures, new ideas, new inspiration, and new strategies that await you.

SCARCITY MENTALITY

Scarcity affects our thinking and increases that feeling of not being enough. It shifts our mind to automatically and powerfully focus on unfulfilled needs. We wonder, "How come I can't get my needs fulfilled?" How many times have you seen a friend get married and think, "They were lucky cause there're no more good men left." What you're saying and also doing is focusing on lack and hypothesizing that there aren't many opportunities left. The biggest problem with embracing a scarcity mentality is that it puts you into the victim mindset. It takes away your position of control over the situation. It makes you hustle harder to secure the bag. We ruminate, stress, complain, and fixate, reinforcing the underlying false belief that there must be something wrong with us if we don't have this "thing." If you are engaging in the following, you're operating in the scarcity mindset:

- Complaining and Gossiping
- Discontentment and Frustration
- Worrying and Fixating
- Hustling and Hoarding
- Feeling Jealous and Comparing

Comparison also leads me to focus on fear. I'm fearful that I'm missing out on what I could have or what I should be doing. We're also afraid that in being our authentic self, we will be judged as lame, boring, and, you guessed it, just not good enough. This component of comparison will always have you wanting to be someone else, trying to erase yourself and shape into something else. It puts you into the vulnerable state of admitting that rejection and hurt is possible, and honestly, it's a time thief. We waste time in our one precious life by hoping to be something other than ourselves.

How many moments in life have you missed out on because you weren't able to fully appreciate it because something else was missing? How many years has discontentment stolen from you, believing that a relationship would be your true source of happiness? I've been there, and I can say it's taken me over ten years to release discontentment from my life. Even then, it still rears its ugly head.

One time, I was looking cute on vacation with great weather and good food. It was a week-long retreat meant for restoration and relaxation. I was spending as much time as possible every day on the beach: I did morning sunrise runs, talked to God, and gained insight about my future and all the wonderful things to come. I got amazing downloads for my vision the following year. I felt rejuvenated and had new energy to produce and create.

Later that week I got on good ol' social media. I was just scrolling along, liking pictures, and responding. Then I saw a friend of mine.

We basically became each other's personal therapist for five years straight. We were both going through divorces at the same time.

Our whole lives were falling apart—together. We helped each other through our traumatic times and spent hours talking, texting, just going out, and being each other's support. As we started to heal, our lives recovered in different ways.

She found a boyfriend and got engaged and married. I got a new job, a promotion, and I moved out of the state. I remember us talking during this period of change, and we were both genuinely happy for each other. As my career progressed, she expressed that she felt she should've been further along by now. She was comparing herself to my career success: landing the new job, making a lot more money, winning national awards, and getting promoted. I affirmed her progress and told her that she was on the right path to what mattered most to her, and there's nothing wrong with that.

Lo and behold, it was my turn to bite the comparison bullet. I was on social media and now I saw that she was having a baby.

Cue comparison pattern. She and I were at the same bad place at the same time. Our lives went in two different directions. One thing I realized as we compared ourselves against each other is that you have no idea what someone's priority truly is. I may have said that having a healthy relationship, getting married, and having children was a priority, but I also wanted to be successful. I wanted to be self-sufficient, own real estate, and make good money. But the fact of the matter is that my true priority was what I succeeded in and the same goes for her.

The problem was that while I was comparing myself to my friend and looking at her progress versus my progress, I began to dismiss and belittle how far I've come on my journey. To be clear, her goals were completely different than mine. When I compared myself to her, I took my goals and my accomplishments and threw them in the trash. I told myself that I still wasn't good enough because I wasn't able to achieve what she has. That's why it's imperative to appreciate and measure your success based upon yourself and your priorities.

FEAR

Fear is at the root of our need to compare ourselves. As I stated at the beginning of this chapter, we use comparison to benchmark ourselves against others, using them as an evaluation tool for our progress. Fear enters when we benchmark ourselves against someone else and feel that we've come up inadequate. This fear opens the door to impostor syndrome, self-hatred, unworthiness, insecurities, and more. Yet if we look at fear correctly, its goal is to protect us. In the early development of humans, it was a vital emotional response to physical or emotional danger in order to avoid life or death consequences.

But feeling inadequate because a friend makes more money than you is not an immediate threat of danger, but fear is still at the root. This fear starts when we analyze our friends and evaluate ourselves against them. For example, you may think, "We both have the same degree and graduated school around the same time, and although she went the intern route and was paid less while I went into an administrative position, she's somehow surpassed me." With this thought process, it then becomes apparent to you that the financial space and career promotions your friend is enjoying should also be what you're enjoying. Since you haven't attained those heights, then you must be a loser. The fear here is that you haven't grown and prospered in a manner as someone with similar choices as you.

Now having identified this fear, you understand that this evaluation is a morphed form of protection. But you don't need protection. There is no real danger in making less, but the idea that you may have taken the wrong path in life is no less alarming. The first thing I want to say here is that in trying to protect ourselves, we also oversimplify our comparisons and do not understand that life is not binary. Things can change and the route in which your friend may have achieved her growth and promotion is not the only way to reach that goal. You are not worse off nor better off than your friend, just different than your friend. Assigning value to yourself based on the unknown variables of your friend doesn't provide any true meaning, and it distracts you from living your life in this moment. To be fair, you don't know what beautiful life-changing moments you may have never experienced going the exact route as your friend. If you believe in the path you've chosen, you'll understand that you can achieve what you desire in multiple ways.

HOW TO PROCESS COMPARISON

Do not determine your worth based on what somebody else is good at. Everybody has different skills, talents, and abilities and goals that may or may not be equal to you. Their passion, intensity, and tenacity might also be different. The best way to evaluate your progress is to look at your past state and compare your progress to yourself. Have you accomplished your goals? Do you see emotional growth? What are your priorities and are your actions supporting what you desire to achieve?

Connection not comparison

Look for connection, not comparison. I commented on my friend's announcement of her pregnancy and she immediately responded. That helped me get out of my feelings. We were able to chat a little bit and catch up on both of our lives, and it closed the gap on what I thought was so different and out of reach for me.

When you get the urge to compare yourself to a friend, reach out to connect instead. If you admire her business or her beautiful connections, it could be an opportunity to connect and ask questions. You can learn how she did it and in what ways you could apply her strategies to get similar results.

Appreciate your differences

Recognize that you are not the same. Do not put yourself in their category. I don't care if it's your friend, sister, or cousin. It doesn't matter if you are the same age, same size, same height, same weight, same skin color, or have the same income. I don't care what it is; you are not the same. You have different experiences growing up, even in the same home. Your personality is different. Your disposition, your mannerisms, your goals are all different. So when you compare yourself to others, it's like comparing carrots to oranges. It's harder to extract carrot juice from a carrot than it is to extract orange juice from an orange. Although they're both orange, good for you, and tasty, they have to be processed differently to extract the juice. The same concept applies to you. Your life circumstance will bring out gifts and abilities that are unique to you, and we all have to be processed in our own way. That's the only way they could have come about.

Start a gratitude practice

Practicing gratitude puts you into a receiving state. You will begin to notice what has gone well, realize the growth you've made, and celebrate the accomplishments and other achievements that have now manifested. It shifts us from a scarcity mindset into a mindset of abundance:

- There is more than enough.
- I have enough.
- I am enough.
- I am all of what I need.
- Life happens for me not against me.

An abundance mindset allows us to see our present life with appreciation, to trust ourselves, and bring peace to our progress and our relationships. If you spent every evening jotting down just three things you were grateful for, it would help you shift into abundance and away from focusing on lack. Remember, what you focus on, you expand.

Honor the sacredness of your season

You were not meant to be in summer and spring at all times. It's out of the natural order of life. Embrace the season you are in because that's where you can find the most joy and contentment. Self-compassion is the key to honoring your sacred season. The growth you desire, the results you want—all of it happens in your current season. All you have is the now: what's presently in front of you. When we waste our time rejecting our season wishing for another, we do not honor the life we've been given. This is time that we can never get back. Thus, it's best to learn and accomplish what you can in the season so you can reap the most results when your following season arrives. Be patient with yourself. You are a masterpiece in progress.

POINTS TO PONDER

I encourage you to practice these four steps:

1. Look for a way to connect and not compare.
2. Embrace your unique difference.
3. Start a practice of gratitude.
4. Honor your sacred season.

Try to remember one or two of these so when you start to compare yourself to people on social media or to friends or family that have achieved things you wanted, you have a plan to intercept those thoughts. Comparison is a time thief. When we spend time wishing and hoping to become something else or live as someone else, we make our happiness a fleeting goal. We have to embrace the time we have, being accountable for our actions, and realize that happiness is our own responsibility.

CHAPTER 14

LONELINESS—BUT I LOVE MYSELF

When I was younger, I frequently suffered from feeling lonely. I had family, but I never really had deep, lasting connections with friends. The friendships would be based on work, or school, my time at an organization, or church activities. As soon as those activities changed, I no longer had those people as friends. So I was in search of finding a lasting friendship. What I realize now is that the void that I was looking to fulfill in friendship was myself. I was trying to fill a void that should have started with embracing me.

Since I didn't always understand that, I spent a lot of time being inauthentic to try to make friends. I became the friend that I thought they needed me to be. I sought out their approval and their love while denying my values and my needs. It wasn't until I got comfortable being alone that I stopped feeling lonely. Loneliness has nothing to do with who is around: it's all about you. I know this because I have been married before but still felt lonely. The root of my loneliness wasn't about someone else bringing me external stimulation; it was more about my internal experience and condition.

But it wasn't just me. I found that a study conducted by Cigna stated that two in five Americans have said that they sometimes are lonely or feel their social relationships are not meaningful. In addition, a Kaiser Family Foundation / Economist survey found that one in five say they feel lonely or socially isolated. Now loneliness is a personal experience that varies from person to person and can be caused by life events that include:

- Experiencing grief and loss
- Breaking up with a friend or significant other
- Changing jobs and feeling isolated from your co-workers
- Starting a new school
- Moving to a new location without community support from family and friends
- Experiencing loneliness during holidays like Valentine's Day or Christmas

In addition to life events, we can also experience loneliness if we are a part of specific groups or excluded from groups, such as being estranged from your family and being the black sheep.

Maybe you are a single parent, experiencing a financial hardship, and unable to attend social activities that your married friends can afford.

WHAT IS LONELINESS?

It can be described as pain from isolation or separation and can be accompanied by frustration, sadness, sorrow, and anger.

Loneliness may be a form of self-protection. You may have chosen it to avoid humiliation and embarrassment. Or it can be caused by shyness, social anxiety, sensitivity, or rejection.

You can experience two types of loneliness: a shorter period of loneliness caused by a specific situation or chronic loneliness that tends to last much longer. Experiencing loneliness on a chronic basis is usually based on personal factors like feeling inadequate and insecure. I've experienced both types of loneliness in my life. For example, I had a very close loved one pass away. After his death, I felt that there was a hole in my life. Something greatly missing caused a deep loneliness within me. That type of loneliness may be shorter, but it was complicated. It required me to resolve my grief before I could alleviate my loneliness and form new social relationships. I've also experienced loneliness during my marriage and during the divorce. During that chronic loneliness, I had to work on feelings of personal inadequacy and insecurity.

One of the biggest obstacles to overcoming loneliness is building resistance to it. We resist embracing, understanding, or acknowledging that we are lonely. Instead, we blame the people around us for our loneliness. Four years after my loved one passed away, I was still blaming him for feeling lonely. I convinced myself that my feelings of loneliness were his fault because how I was currently living was not the way it was supposed to be. We made plans, and he was supposed to be around forever. No matter how painful it was, I couldn't address the loneliness until I addressed the grief.

IMPACT OF LONELINESS

Many people deny their loneliness. They hide it or run away from it because they are ashamed to admit that they're in pain and feel a stigma. They don't want to acknowledge it publicly, or even to themselves. Instead, they say things like, "There are no good men around," "My friends are trash," or "It's just hard for me to connect to anyone." When we reject our loneliness and run from it and then blame other people for it, we end up engaging in a vicious cycle.

I was placing my loneliness in the lap of other people and expecting an external source to comfort me. I modified my behavior so I could avoid loneliness and have friends. In an effort to fill an empty gap and avoid the fear of being alone, I started seeking approval from other people. Filling the gap in with people around me just led me into a rejection cycle.

With my fear of being alone, I sought the approval of other people to become my friend. I then overextended myself, and if my overextension was received and I got approval, it reinforced my pattern. However, if I overextended myself and it was not received or appreciated and I did not get approval, I felt rejected. It reinforced my fear of being alone and made me want to try harder. The end result was that I found myself doing things not because I wanted to but because someone else wanted me to. I began shrinking my ideas and my desires to fit the pattern of other people so they could be accepted and I could feel accepted.

It caused my true identity to be challenged, and to some degree, I lost a part of myself by continuously adjusting to what other people liked. We all seek acceptance, belonging, and finding a place where we feel we truly belong. But if you are around the wrong people, this can be manipulated, those desires perverted, and our identity stripped.

Feelings of loneliness signal to us that we are looking for connection and meaning. From a primitive perspective, it was how we survived and thrived. The feeling of loneliness encouraged connection to be a part of the human group and to survive and find a role and meaning within that group. Loneliness signals us to the potential of personal growth and new possibilities. It can motivate us to grow, explore, and come out of our shell to appreciate the supporters of our needs.

HOW TO OVERCOME LONELINESS

Loneliness opens the door to discontentment and comparison.

Because my identity was based on what others wanted and I acquiesced, or adapted, to their hobbies and interests to keep them happy, my identity was up for grabs the moment friendship was offered. I had to get clear on my core values and my personal principles. Our core values help us create boundaries and align our daily activities and behavior with our purpose, thus creating an intentionally joyful life.

Core value system

Operating from a firm foundation and value system made the difference on how much I would engage or address potential relationships. This helped me stay grounded and emotionally sober. In the past, it was easy for me to become drunk off of other people's approval. It was my high and go-to for fixing and boosting my self- esteem. But once I got clear on my identity, I decided I would honor everything about who I am and the life I am living. That meant making decisions to nourish my body, my mind, and my soul with people and places that nourish me deeply. Getting in alignment with my identity was the biggest game changer. I spent time evaluating my core values and life goals and determined that if anyone came into my life violating either of those, that person was not meant to be part of my future. It was tough at first to turn down friends that were seemingly decent relationships, but I know allowing myself to be connected to them would deplete me in the long run. It was simple but took time.

To find my core values and determine whom I would let in, I looked at my current friends. Early on, I used to gather friends that needed a friend because I like to be inclusive; it's my nature. Unfortunately, more than once I allowed their needs to supersede mine. They would consistently share their stories, request help, and want to meet up when they were in need, but when the tables were turned and I needed help, their cup would be empty. They had nothing to share with me and nothing to give in return.

I couldn't blame them for this response because I allowed them to take more than they gave consistently. I didn't speak up when I needed something or voice my displeasure in their lack of reciprocation. I felt that because I was the stronger one in the friendship that it was OK; I could handle it alone. I was hiding my feelings and some of my friends were making more emotional withdrawals from the friendship than deposits. From those experiences, I realized that two of the values I needed from my friends were dependability and trust. Knowing that I can trust someone with the deep pains of my heart and they'll actually be there for me in that moment became a non-negotiable requirement of future friendships.

Living in purpose

I had to address my insecurities of seeking approval and following the rejection cycle. I had to let down my walls. I had to get clear on my purpose and spend more time in self-discovery to understand the vision I wanted to manifest in my life. Your purpose is your companion, and it will organically draw like-minded people to your life. However, if you're unaware of your purpose or are running from it, you will embrace and connect with people that will become distractions or hindrances to your progress.

Connecting with people in this state will only amplify your loneliness. It wasn't until I decided to get serious about my purpose to help women transform their lives emotionally and financially that I started to attract friends that were of a similar mindset. The loneliness I found when I was living outside of my purpose came because I was trying to connect with people who did not have a drive or desire to change much since they were happy with what they had. And that's OK too, but if I share my goals and vision with my friend, and they can't see beyond their current goals, it would be hard for them not to speak doubt over my plans, and that ultimately slowed me down.

I think we underestimate the value of our purpose, as if it's only an ancillary part of us or an unattainable goal. I believe the desires you have inside of you to create the business, paint the canvas, or write the song were given to you as your gift. It's your meaning for living. If we treat it as "just something I'm good at doing," we block ourselves from being able to see the benefits that will unfold if we stay faithful to perfecting our craft. The distractions we engage in only dilute and destroy our confidence and endurance. We miss out on turning our potential into progress while sitting on the sidelines. There are people assigned to your purpose that will never manifest if you don't get focused.

POINTS TO PONDER

Loneliness can be described as pain from isolation or separation and can be accompanied by frustration, sadness, sorrow, and anger. It can be chronic or temporary and situation based. Chronic feelings of loneliness can result from feeling inadequate or insecure. To overcome chronic feelings of loneliness, we must start with our feelings of inadequacy, seek to understand our identity, follow our core values, and find fulfillment in our purpose.

CHAPTER 15

ANXIETY – LET'S GET IT POPPIN'

I was set to sign the papers to become the legal owner of my new apartment building. It was my closing date. This final step was supposed to be a joyous day. I worked so hard to get this house, and it was finally mine. All mine. About two hours before my appointment at the title company, I had a whole panic attack. I was overwhelmed with anxiety when I began to think about how much money I was spending and how much debt I was taking on as a single woman. It freaked me out.

I had never signed a contract for such a large amount of money.

I envisioned myself missing payments, my building being foreclosed, and myself ending up on the streets. I'd be homeless, completely unable to receive help or assistance. I literally saw myself being labeled a failure in life, embarrassed that I even tried. What was I thinking, I'm single? I have no backup plan. There's no one else to support me. If I go down, who's gonna help me? No one can help me.

All of these negative thoughts were firing off in my brain. It turned from irrational thoughts to shortness of breath to my heartbeat rising dramatically. Before I knew it, I burst into tears and fell on the floor. I cried my eyes out. I didn't like owing anyone money and was so afraid of what seemed like an insurmountable amount of debt.

All I could think about was past times when I had experienced loss. I replayed the painful memories of family members having their car repossessed or their home foreclosed upon. I felt like I was signing up for that experience all over again, thinking, *Who am I to think I'll be any different than them?* I contemplated calling my real estate agent and telling him, "I'm backing out of the deal. It's too much money. I can't do it."

The funny thing is, all the way up until the closing date, I was all in, guns blazing! I was focused on saving money and began eating more meals at home, taking my lunch to work, doing my own nails, and doing my own hair. I saved every dollar I could so I could afford this home. But, on the day of closing, I lost it. I allowed anxiety to take over. Thank goodness, in the middle of me bawling on the floor, I got a phone call, it must have been God. A friend called me to congratulate me and to see how I was doing before the closing appointment. They could hear my sniffling and asked if I was crying. I tried to fake it at first, but then I burst into tears all over again. I just let it all come out, and I told them how I was really feeling.

My friend told me to first stand up and take deep breaths. He reminded me that I had made it this far and how much I always wanted my own home. He assured me that no one would loan me money, after going through a rigorous underwriting process, if they thought that I couldn't afford it. "You passed the test; all you have to do now is get your reward." He helped shift my thinking from thoughts of panic, worst-case scenario, disaster, and doom to "You deserve this. You wanted to be a real estate mogul. This is your first step. Celebrate yourself." His response helped change my entire perspective of how I dealt with anxiety from that day forward.

Anxiety is the feeling of fear about what's to come and can exist for multiple reasons. Our biased thinking can provide fuel to the anxiety. If we believe we were born to struggle, or fight, or be taken advantage of, our thinking will support our anxiety in that way. We overestimate how bad the outcome will be and start catastrophizing or imagining the worst. If we don't have our negative thoughts under control, anxiety fused with negative thoughts and overestimation can send us on a downward spiral.

Anxiety can be triggered by the following:

- Conflicts at Work, School, or Home
- Social Events
- Phobias
- Memories of Traumatic Events
- Health Issues such as Diabetes, Asthma, or Irritable Bowel Syndrome
- Money Management
- Caffeine
- Medications

How we process information can also have an impact on our anxiety. If you tend to selectively look for information that supports your worry and reduce or ignore any evidence that refutes it, your perspective can increase anxiety. Have you ever had a headache and convinced yourself it was a brain tumor after a few minutes on a medical website? I know many people feel that a lot of their anxiety comes from past experiences, mainly their memories. We can experience mild anxiety in the back of our mind as we go throughout our daily activities or have an anxiety attack that is disruptive and severe. The behavioral techniques we engage in to cope with our anxiety can vary, but here are a few behaviors we use as a form of safety:

- Avoidance of anything that provokes anxiety
- Aggression, verbal abuse, lashing out
- Alcohol and/or drug use
- Compulsive behaviors, harmful rituals, or routines

The loop starts as a fearful thought, and then anxiety response, and then taking action with a safety behavior (avoidance, aggression, alcohol, or compulsive behaviors). We find ourselves in this continuous cycle every time our anxiety is triggered.

IMPACT OF ANXIETY

Anxiety impacts our relationships and our decisions and often manifests itself physiologically. I had a friend that used to become anxious as soon as she would get into a relationship. She often worried about how she responded to him through text or whether something she said would cause the end of their relationship.

Because she wanted to ensure the connection remained intact, she usually splurged on gifts for him and ways she could make him happy. If he was feeling tired or just not wanting to talk that day, my friend would assume their relationship was coming to an end soon and overanalyze and replay every word in the conversation. She lost sleep, time, and occasionally, her appetite, and it wasn't until she read a book on attachment styles that she started to realize her behavior (and by "her," I mean me, lol).

My relationships

In the book *Attached: The New Science of Adult Attachment and How It Can Help You Find—and Keep—Love*, I learned that of the four relationship attachment styles, I had an anxious attachment in relationships. This meant that I greatly craved intimacy, which drove feelings of neediness, preoccupation with the relationship, and worry about people close to me loving me back. I preferred my significant other to be in close proximity and wrestled with the anxiety of abandonment.

I can't say I was too happy when I read that. In fact, it made me a little angry, and I rejected it at first. But the more I read the book, the examples, and the supporting science, it was hard to refute that I was anything else. I examined my past relationships and the repeating cycles I had endured and ultimately created, and had to say, "Yup, that's me." Here are some ways the book mentions anxious attachment style that can be exhibited in your behavior:

You worry that your partner may not like the real you and stop loving you.

You get anxious about expressing your feelings to your partner because you fear they won't feel the same way.

You tend to get attached to a romantic partner very quickly and think about your relationships a lot.

If your partner's mood changes, you're sensitive to it and begin to wonder if you've done something wrong.

I can say I've acted out 90 percent of this list in a relationship before. One positive aspect that the book highlights for people that have an anxious attachment style is our unique ability to sense when something is wrong in the relationship. I can definitely sense it early on in the relationship, but the problem is that any slight hint that something is wrong triggers the anxious attachment system. It would take a while for me to be calmed down until I received clear reassurance from my partner that the relationship is safe. If I never received that assurance, then I was in a constant state of anxiety about our future. It was daunting.

Decision-making

Anxiety can also hijack your decision-making process. The goal of anxiety is to direct our behavior to the safest possible option. It is necessary to help us move cautiously and avoid quick decisions that lead to failure, but at times, it can be overbearing and get in the way of making big progress in your life.

When it comes to making decisions, anxiety intercepts the process of the prefrontal cortex, the area of the brain that is responsible for helping us weigh consequences, plan, and process thoughts in a logical way. It helps defuse the emotion out of a decision by calming the amygdala. A study done by the University of Pittsburg found that anxiety selectively shuts down those connections, which makes it more difficult for the brain to screen out irrelevant information in order for us to make better decisions.

This is exactly what happened when I had my anxiety attack before signing the closing documents for my apartment building. All rational and logical options were excluded from my thinking, and all I could focus on were the worst-case scenarios of losing my building and ultimately becoming homeless and a complete failure in life. I laugh now when I think about it, but at the time, it was as real to me as the ground I stood on.

Physiological response

Anxiety can manifest in our bodies as an attack to include a racing heartbeat, shortness of breath, tightness in the throat, sweating, nausea, headaches, and feeling faint or dizzy. As you're experiencing the anxiety, the body's autonomous fight-or-flight response takes over and generates all these physical symptoms. Tuning into your body's typical response will be a cue for you to intercept your anxiety response. This is how you become the director of the story and put yourself back in charge.

In my body, worry, excitement, and anxiety manifest in my core: the belly. It can result in stomach and digestive issues. Chronic worry and anxiety tend to settle in my stomach and go up to my abdomen, resulting in poor breathing. Usually, people that suffer from anxiety don't breathe deeply from the diaphragm. Their breathing is shallow and rapid and robs the body of oxygen. For me, it creates an unconscious response to protect myself, curling up into the smallest possible ball and trying to make myself invisible.

This is subconsciously done as my body tries to protect itself from the cruelty of the outside world.

HOW I PROCESS ANXIETY

I developed a fun acronym to help me remember how to handle my anxiety and negative thoughts and remind me to get LIT, which stands for:

- L- Label the anxiety for what it is.
- I- Investigate the fear you are trying to avoid.

- T- Transform the fear into affirmations and take action.

In *labeling* the anxiety for what it is, I need you to get specific and learn to separate the thoughts as a storyline or a movie that likes to play in your head. Give that movie a title or give the character of the story a name. One of my favorite apocalyptic climate change movies is *The Day After Tomorrow,* where the entire world gets hit by a catastrophic natural disaster of epic proportions. I like to name my anxiety-driven thoughts after the movie and I call it, *The Disaster After Tomorrow.* Or in the case of naming the anxiety after a character, I'm reminded of the Allstate insurance company character Mayhem. Mayhem, played by actor Dean Winters, appears in the insurance commercials as a destructive character that represents all the things that could go wrong that you would need insurance for, like wind storms, car accidents, or my favorite, a neighbour accidentally chopping down a tree and it landing on your house.

Labeling helps you identify what's happening rather than embracing it as usual. If you can label it as "oh, that's just my *Disaster After Tomorrow* starting to play," or "that's just Mr. Mayhem popping in," it's easier to identify the anxiety loop as it's happening. Labeling these feelings helps regulate the emotion and promote insight during times of stress and emotional upset. It will help you feel empowered to more effectively deal with the real feeling and issue.

The next part of the acronym is *investigate.* I want you to examine the anxiety thoughts with self-compassion and determine what fear you're trying to avoid. Is it scarcity, abandonment, rejection, or resentment? This helps you get to the real issue. You can explore that emotion and identify the root of what's triggering your feelings. You cannot address or comfort the parts of you that you are unwilling to acknowledge.

Armed with the understanding of your fear, it's time to *transform* that thought. This is the most important step because change will not come until you learn how to shift your thoughts and attention from the intrusive anxiety thoughts that arise. To transform that thought, counter it with a positive affirmation. Remember that you've lived your life focused on negative and limiting beliefs, and as I've said before—what you focus on, you expand. It's expanded so much that it's gotten out of control and made you lose touch with reality. Affirmations help counter those thoughts, and when continuously said over time, they shift your beliefs and your thinking. Take a look at these examples:

Thought	Affirmation
I don't think I'll ever be able to finish school.	I am capable of solving any problems that face me.
I'm not qualified to start a business.	I am always under divine inspiration and I know what to do.
If I say no to their request, they'll reject me.	It is safe for me to speak up for myself.
Something is always going wrong, and I can't catch a break.	Everything is always working out for me.
I'm sick of dating; I'll never find the one.	I am well loved and draw to me my highest good.

Once you have your affirmations set, you need to take action. In the typical anxiety loop, the safety behaviors are avoidance, aggression, alcohol or drug use, or compulsive behavior. We have to counter those actions with an action that reinforces your affirmation. Don't rush yourself, but spend some time thinking about this. Ask yourself, "If worry wasn't present, how would I respond?"

For example, if anxiety was hijacking your decision-making process and you were wondering if you should take the new job or stay where you're at, stop and take some time to write the pros and cons of the new job and talk it over with a friend or loved one.

Getting it out of your head, on paper, and discussing it will help give you insight into your decision. To ultimately shift your thinking, you must change the belief and then take action that reinforces the belief. Actions are the most effective affirmation. Actions shape reality. Next time anxiety thoughts arise, remember to get LIT.

POINTS TO PONDER

Anxiety is the feeling of fear about the future or uncertain situations. When the anxiety loop kicks in, we're prone to execute safety behaviors such as avoidance, aggression, drug or alcohol use, or compulsive behavior. We can counter this loop by getting LIT.

FINAL WORDS

You made it to the end of this book, and I know that you've probably had multiple insights on how to interpret your emotions and effect change in your life. I want to remind you in this growth process to be gentle with yourself as you release old patterns and break limiting habits. I pray that you find a community of love and support that will uplift you in and through this process as you blossom, and may you find the courage to manifest your higher self.

WILL YOU HELP ME?

Thank You For Reading My Book!

If you loved my book, don't forget to leave a review!

Every review matters, and it matters a *lot!*

Head over to Amazon or wherever you purchased this book to leave an honest review for me.

I thank you endlessly.

—Sherese

ABOUT THE AUTHOR

Sherese Shy-Holmes is a speaker, coach, and entrepreneur. Known for her ability to shift women from confusion to clarity in just one conversation, she empowers women with practical strategies that generate results.

With a formal education in business, taxes, and auditing, Sherese uses a no-fluff approach to formulating ideas, developing an action plan, and creating solutions for her life and business coaching clients. She defines herself as the "Business Doula" that helps ambitious, spiritually-minded women monetize their purpose, navigate solo business development, and break their financial glass ceilings.

She is the founder of Empowered to Prosper, whose mission is to foster a rich growth and support community for women to achieve their life and business goals through workshops, women's circles, courses, and coaching.

Blog: https://www.thebizdoula.com

(Click on "Contact Me" to inquire about having Sherese speak at your event)

Podcast: https://healandsell.buzzsprout.com

Instagram: https://www.instagram.com/thebizdoula

Tik Tok: https://www.tiktok.com/@thebizdoula

Facebook: https://www.facebook.com/thebizdoula

www.ingramcontent.com/pod-product-compliance
Lightning Source LLC
Chambersburg PA
CBHW072008290426
44109CB00018B/2180